Parasitic People

Ron Russo

ISBN 978-1-64191-339-3 (paperback)
ISBN 978-1-64191-340-9 (digital)

Copyright © 2018 by Ron Russo

All rights reserved. No part of this publication may be reproduced, distributed, or transmitted in any form or by any means, including photocopying, recording, or other electronic or mechanical methods without the prior written permission of the publisher. For permission requests, solicit the publisher via the address below.

Christian Faith Publishing, Inc.
832 Park Avenue
Meadville, PA 16335
www.christianfaithpublishing.com

Printed in the United States of America

I like to dedicate this book to my sister, Margarita Sorbello, who helped me edit it, but most importantly with her many trials and tribulations displayed the strength to press on with her faith and trust in Jesus Christ.

And to my niece Kimberly Ross, who tragically lost three daughters, yet she believed the Lord would supply her with great blessings. And he did bless her.

And to my other sister, Anna, family, and friends who made it through their darkest hour with hope in their hearts.
Thank you, Jesus.

INTRODUCTION
(Portions from Wikipedia)

Parasitism is a nonmutual symbiotic relationship between species, where one species, the parasite, benefits at the expense of the other, the host.

Unlike predators, parasites typically do not kill their host, are generally much smaller than their host, and will often live in or on their host for an extended period.

Parasites show a high degree of specialization and reproduce at a faster rate than their hosts (i.e., tapeworms, fluke, and fleas).

Parasites reduce the host biological fitness by general or pathological means, such as parasitic castration and impairment of secondary sex characteristics leading to the modification of the host behavior. On the other hand, parasites will increase their fitness by exploiting the host for resources necessary for their survival. This could be attained through water, food, heat, habitat, and transmission.

Parasitism comes from the Greek words *para* and *sitos* which mean "feeding" or "fattening."

In the following chapter, we will cover the different types of parasites and their characteristics, intentions, favorable environment, and how their purpose and lifestyle are shockingly the kind of behavior found in human individuals, seeking a human host to feed off.

In the progressing chapters, you will see the interaction of the victimized host and the battle with parasites. You will see how alcohol, drugs, smoking, and other abusive habits will wear down the host as well as make it more difficult for the parasite to continue maintaining the host until they find a safe haven in another host.

You will see why parasites got that way and what could be done to change their lives into a more productive purposeful existence. You will learn the "should and shouldn't do" part of the host, through Christian standards and principles, a measure of guidelines, and real-life stories.

"Readers View" ronsmaincourt@gmail.com

Chapter 1

The Different Types of Parasites: Comparisons to the Human Personality Creating the Environment or Defenses

Ectoparasites live outside of the host (skin), for example, mites, fleas, and lice.

The ectohumans are the outside influence to the host, maybe they are at the workplace or your favorite bar or night spot. They could be friends or outside relatives. They could be at the store or marketplace you frequently visit. These ectohumans though not in your inner circle could be a threat to your outside world and how you view it and deal with it. Our environment has a profound influence on our behavior, demeanor, and decisions both wise and foolish.

If you are not careful, the ectoparasite will feed on your surroundings, bind up your time and freedom, and weaken your productivity. They will bind up your priorities and confuse or tie up your plans for the day, week, month, and sometimes years.

You can find them if you move into a bad neighborhood or if you get involved in a hobby or social group. Sometimes we are forced into an environment that we feel uneasy about or insecure, such as a job relocation in an undesirable area. Sometimes we create an environment that we think will work well for us but later find out that the ectohumans surround us.

It is like the old saying, "Tell me whom your friends are, and I will tell you to what you are likened." In many cases, this is so true.

Notwithstanding the land shall be desolate because of them that dwell therein, for the fruit of their doings. (Micah 7:13)

The Defense

Like, when the ectoparasites like lice attack the skin, how you build up the skin with vitamins to make the skin tough and waterproof and make the pH level acidic which kills most parasites, build your acid fortress to keep the desolate people out. Defend your outside surroundings.

Endoparasites live inside the host such as bacteria or a virus. They sometime rely on a third party to be a carrier or vector such as mosquitos.

The endoparasite can severely affect the overall health of the host. They attack the muscles and joints and body parts and cause pain and discomfort. They slow you down and hinder your mobility. They clutter your head with teary eyes and clogged sinuses and popping ear sounds. They give the host a headache and cloud the mind so the host can't think properly.

Endopeople are the ones that get into your inner circle, often a family member or a so-called friend who weaves his or her lifestyle into the host to influence decisions and actions of the host for the friend you can't ignore, for fear of offending your good friend or family member.

The endopeople will sap your strength, time, ambitions, and dreams. They are capable of giving you a nervous breakdown and break you down physically.

Proceed with caution when an endoperson is introduced to you. If you have any suspicions about the friend of a friend, then pay attention to your heart. Be courteous and tell them to have a good time, and you have to get back to your business.

Mesoparasites are half outside and half inside.

The mesopeople will affect your inner circle and your world around you. They have all the characteristics of the ectoparasite and endoparasite together in combination. They affect and exploit the host from every angle.

> *Let them be ashamed and confounded that seek after my soul: Let them be turned backward, and put to confusion, that desire my hurt.* (Psalm 70:2)

Epiparasites are a parasite that feeds, that is, a parasite living in the digestive tract of a flea living on a dog, in other words an endoparasite (inside) of an ectoparasite (outside) living on a host.

Epipeople depend and feed on other parasitic people who feed off a host. This is a happy arrangement where one person feeds off another person who is feeding on yet another person (the host).

Social parasites are termites and ants.

Social parasitic people gather in numbers to live and eat in a flophouse (community center) where they are happy with free three hots and a cot, always looking for that free handout.

Kleptoparasites appropriate food and labor gathered by the host. Cuckoos and cowbirds do not build nests of their own and leave their eggs in nests of other species. The host becomes a babysitter so to speak raising the young as their own unaware. If the host removes the cuckoos' eggs, some cuckoos will return and attack the nest to compel the host to remain subject to this parasitism (hostage).

I really don't need to teach further on the kleptoperson. They are simply criminal people who pop out babies and dump them with their parents or family member.

> *I will go and return to my place till they acknowledge their offenses and seek my face: In their affliction they will seek me early.* (Hosea 5:15)

An example of *intraspecific social parasitism* is of one nursing female taking milk from other unrelated females. In other words, these high-ranking wedge-capped capuchin females sometimes take milk from lower-ranking females without any return favors or reciprocation. So the high-ranking females will benefit at the expense of low-ranking females.

Miss Intraperson is like two women in the kitchen so to speak—the roommate or friend who exercises and flaunts her superiority, looks, charm, and acceptance over her host-like girlfriend. Ladies, you don't need friends like that.

Parasitism is a term which describes the role of isolated cheating or exploitation among the more generalized mutualistic interactions. An example of this is two different species sharing the same environment, like plants and fungi exchanging carbon and nutrients in a common mutualistic relationship. The problem is that some plant species known as myco-heterotrophs are "cheaters," meaning instead of donating carbon, they take it from the fungus.

Parapeople by hook or crook take as much as they can from whomever they can and whenever they can and make little contribution or sacrifice in return. They take advantage of the resources and waste rather than conserve.

Now that we have a general idea of the different types of parasites in relation to their hosts and the comparisons with the human host and parasite, we proceed to looking at some of the host defenses outlined in the next section.

Host Defenses

I will first introduce to you what real parasites do to the skin, mouth, stomach, eyes, and immune system and how to prevent them. I will follow up with the human parasite in contrast to the damage done to the host and how to combat it.

Skin

This is the first line of defense against invading parasites. The skin has several layers containing keratin protein which makes skin tough and waterproof. Parasites need a moist environment to survive. In the human application, just like the wet skin creates an environment for parasites, compare if you will water weeds instead of the flowers.

Safeguard against these invaders by not allowing them to get on your skin. They will make your life uncomfortable. They are *itching* to invade your life and will cause *flakiness*. They will make you *red* with anger. Be wise and think before you allow people like these into your life.

> *For wisdom is a defense and money is a defense: but the excellency of knowledge is that wisdom giveth life to them that have it.* (Ecclesiastes 7:12)

Mouth

The saliva prevents parasites from entering the body orally. The mouth also contains enzymes to break down the cell walls of invading microorganisms. Without that protection, the mouth is an open pit for invaders. With humans, don't gossip or you will be the victim of gossip. Stay away from gossiping parasites that spew the parasites out of their mouth into some parasitic ear.

> *Keep thy tongue from evil, and thy lips from speaking guile.* (Psalm 34:13)

Stomach

If these parasites get past the mouth, the stomach is the next line of defense. The stomach contains gastric acid (hydrochloric acid) which is around a pH level of 2. The acids will kill most microorganisms, but some are resistant and invade the body through the intestinal tract. Poison might be tasted or detected in the mouth without possible fatal consequences, but once ingested in the stomach, the chances of survival are slim.

Application

You know the old saying, "Junk in, junk out." When we eat something bad, we usually get bad consequences. Healthy food produces a healthy body. With parasitic people, they are not only careless of what they put in their stomach but will also coax you into the same abusiveness. Have one of my cigarettes; have another beer with me; let's get high on drugs, etc. I have a saying, "When you drink with drinkers, you will regret the party." Another way of putting it is "I would rather eat crumbs with my Lord than steak with the devil." At one time or another, we all are faced with pitfalls from childhood to teen years to adulthood. The bitter results vary in degrees and are a hard lesson learned which could be corrected, when wisdom is applied. In other cases, it could cause irreversible damage lasting a lifetime. Figuratively, it is not just what we ingest in our stomach but also what we ingest in our mind, body, and spirit.

The meek shall eat and be satisfied: they shall praise the Lord that seek him: your heart shall live for ever. (Psalm 22:26)

The Eyes
Parasites can invade the body through the eyes. The eyelashes help keep dust and microorganisms from entering the eyes. Tears contain lysozyme (an enzyme) which is able to kill most invading organisms.

Application
You've heard the saying "The eyes are the window to the soul." This is somewhat true in that your inner sense can pick up vibes from another person just by the way that they look at you. Some parasitic people are so demonized that they can't look at you straight in the eyes but rather look to the side of you or worse yet they look through you like you are invisible and they are looking at the wall behind you. They will also distract you by drawing your attention to lustful, greedy, envious, meaningless things. The parasitic eyes almost never shed tears but often produce tears in the host.

Tears kill microorganisms. Tears could mean sadness, remorse, regret, compassion, repentance, overjoyed with happiness, or just plain dirt in the eye. With the exception of the dirt in the eye, the other reasons show the heart. Parasitic people lack these attributes, unless they dramatically fake it. Tears will reveal the heart of a person. During America's involvement in Desert Storm, I remember General Schwarzkopf leading his soldiers into the war and out of the war safely. When his men came back alive, he shed a few tears. A newscaster on the scene mocked him saying, "What is a big military general like you doing crying?" I am not quoting the general's verbatim, but he said something like this: "I am crying because my men came back safely and they could return to their families and loved ones. I would not trust a man that didn't cry." The newscaster was silent. We will learn more about how parasitic people evolve.

Chapter 2

Evolutionary Aspects of Parasitic People

Plant Defenses

Plants undergo a series of metabolic and biochemical reactions creating pathways that will enact a defensive response. Once the plant's receptors recognize the invading parasites, the plant creates defensive compounds to that localized invaded area and induces a hypersensitive response.

Fruit tree farmers spray the trees with chemical that will ward off invading parasites so the outside surface of the fruit looks flawless and has eye appeal in the supermarket. Fruit that grows in the backyard or wild in the field may taste just as good, but is not plump and juicy and eye appealing as the farm raised.

Just like the farmer who fertilizes, waters, prunes, and sprays the fruit trees to produce a healthy growing environment, we must create a healthy environment against parasitic people who invade the host with parched unhallowed ground, the weeds choking out the roots of the fruit tree or plant. The weeds produce other parasites that attack the fruit. If the farmers safeguard against these invaders, they often overcome the obstacles and have a good yield.

Sometimes the enemy will take a battle every now and then, and we suffer loss, but persistence and patience can lead to fruitfulness again.

PARASITIC PEOPLE

In 2014, invading parasites caused a greening on the orange orchards in Florida cutting production in less than half.

> *But he that receiveth seed into the good ground is he that heareth the word, and understandeth it; which also bears fruit, and brings forth fruit, some 100, some 60, and some 30 fold.* (Matthew 13:23)

As many as half of all animals have a parasitic phase in their life cycle. It may be one or many independent parasites. Almost all of free-living animals will be host to at least one and possibly many parasites.

Free-Living Animals

Hmmmmmm free-living parasitic people. What a close comparison. Free sex, multiple partners, free to roam from place to place. There's a song that came out in the early 1960s with the lines "It's your thing. Do watcha wanna do. I can't tell you who to sock it to." The song carried a spirit with it that is very prevalent in our twenty-first century. It is so easy to pick up a disease in a community circle that spreads at a rapid rate. Parasites produce quickly and have a shorter life span, so they act quickly to make their mark before they pass on. Does that sound familiar? Parasites adapt quickly to their environment which gives them an advantage over the slower-moving host.

What Good Can Come from Parasites

It builds the immune system by activating anti-bodies to combat the invading viruses, that is, inoculations for say a flu vaccine. A little of the viral strain is injected to enforce the immune system to resist multiple invading organisms. A farmer told me that he chewed the leaves of a poison ivy plant to build resistance to the plant.

The late televangelist Robert Schuller had a saying, "Turn your scars into stars." Scar tissue could take more of a beating than the normal skin.

Killer Parasites

These are aggressive microorganisms that mutate to survive. They change their characteristics and genetic code that will effectively make them survive. That is, yearly flu vaccines are constantly modified to resist different strains of microorganisms.

Killer Parasitic People

These people will modify their behavior, makeup, demeanor, look, lifestyle, and views to win your acceptance of them. They are the chameleons that seductively blend in. When they make a complete end of you, they will quickly move onto the next host. This is the first type of killer.

Second Killer

They are the multi-host invaders that blend with as many people as they can to support their excessive addictions and self-destructive view of life. They are wise in the world, but fools that live in a world of glitter and lies. There is no discipline or self-control. They use and abuse themselves and others. There is no respect in their understanding. They are compulsive and unteachable. They get bored easily and need constant excitement and entertainment. They get very little sleep, and when they do, they pass out almost to a catatonic state. Then they suddenly wake up and clutter their mind with indulgence and never give themselves quiet time to soberly meditate and reflect on the mild, gentle, and peaceful moment of the day or night.

Defense

The volume of this book will illustrate the number of ways you can deal with this most dangerous parasitic personality. It takes *team* effort to nullify this strain. Have others cooperate with you to get these individuals professional help and tough love and to get legal means to put them in jail, halfway house, church, or institution. This would save them and you.

Ecology

Webster says that ecology is the branch of biology that deals with the relations between living organisms and their environment.

Quantitative ecology concurs that most hosts harbor few parasites, while a few hosts carry a vast majority. So a single parasite species has an aggregated distribution across host individuals. The balance of nature is so intricate and complex that it baffles the scientific community on how codependent relationships depend on one another to complete a life cycle.

The Dung Beetle

My college biology professor was quite a storyteller. He told factual stories with a great deal of humor and fanaticism. The dung beetle is a bug that rolls the dung droppings of a specific animal, breaking the feces up and mixing the feces into the soil. Now the cow dung beetle is specifically designed to handle cow dung. If the cow dung beetle didn't exist, the pasture would burn up and stifle the grass from growing. Thus, the cows would have no food to eat and would starve to death. So this tiny little critter has the most important job of getting his crap together (pun intended). Here is the interesting part of the story. The US Agricultural Department wanted to introduce beef to Australia which would create a new market to that country. The problem with that was there were marsupial dung beetles that could not handle the cow dung. So now the pasture was burning up from all the plops of unprocessed dung in the field. Now the scientists decided that they would transport good old American dung beetles there to clean up the mess. The nearby ponds had frogs, and guess what new delicacy they discovered? You guessed it—cow dung beetles!!!

Now the pasture was plagued by a vast number of frogs feasting on the American cow dung beetle until they were diminished. The scientists put their minds together and came up with the idea that if they import elephant dung beetles from Africa to Australia, these beetles could handle the similar soft plop of cows as they did with elephants. The elephant dung beetle is too large for frogs to eat. In fact, these beetles are so large and powerful that if you held one in your clutched hand, they would force your fingers apart. The scientists were impressed by how well these beetles were cleaning up the cow pies. The problem now was the frogs were determined to eat these new supersized delicacies at any risk. What happens next was that the frogs managed to swallow the beetles, but the beetles walked through their intestinal tract and burst out the frogs' rear end.

It didn't end there. Now they had to clean up a mess of dead frogs which upset the balance of the pond. It went on and on for years before they could create a new environment and ecosystem to be compatible with the marsupial animals such as the kangaroo with the beef cattle.

Every *ecosystem* is unique to the surrounding environment. All living things have a purpose in life. Some creatures like bats are narrowly looked upon as rodents with wings. Did you know that bats each day consume seven times their body weight in bugs? If it were not for the bats, the planet would be plagued with pestilence. In New Jersey universities, they are trying to save the bats from a fungus that is depleting them.

Ecosystems

In a similar way I outlined the problem scientists had with that bizarre dung beetle story, I had my own little problem when making a pond habitat in the side yard of my Woodbury Heights home in New Jersey. In my plastic-lined 10' × 20' × 2 1/2' deep pond, I put potted hybrid water lilies of five or six varieties. I made a beautiful rock garden with colorful foliage around it. I made this cascading 6-foot waterfall with statue and ornaments and a powerful pump/filter. I added koi and goldfish and comets and cats. I created this beautiful little habitat just like in the movie *Field of Dreams* with Kevin Costner, where he built a baseball stadium in the middle of nowhere and drew people from all over. Well not just like it, the theme of the story line was "Build it and they will come." Sure enough as the water lilies grew and started to flower, the dragonflies appeared. The funny thing I have to mention about dragonflies is growing up as a young boy moving into the country from Philadelphia, my mother told me to stay away from dragonflies because they will sew your lips shut. I think my mother's psychology was to protect me from insects that might bite or sting me. It wasn't until I became a teenager that I found out that my mom told me a fable. In any event, I witnessed a colorful variety of beautiful harmless dragonflies and butterflies pollinating the lilies and flowers. Along came frogs and turtles from a lake a block away. Chipmunks moved into the little crevices of the rock garden. My little eco world began to thrive with life and little aquatic organisms, snails, etc. I even had a couple of geese which mate there. All was well, and I spent hours of meditation and prayer there and was so fascinated with watching nature in all its glory which gave me a dazzling show, featuring new shows each day. Then, the "unexpected visitors" appeared.

Unexpected Visitors

You see I made this habitat and other organisms came in to both complete and complement the ecosystem. However, the system was so inviting that snakes and turtles and muskrats and a big blue heron found a new environment to dwell and feast in. I noticed the blue heron was perched on the roof of a neighboring house looking with great intent at the movement within the pond. Within less than a week, that heron snatched about fifty or sixty fish out of my pond. Among the delicacies was my beautiful expensive koi. I let my rottweiler out often to patrol the pond and bark away the heron. The dog and I succeeded in discouraging the heron from returning. Shortly after, I had snapping turtles find their way into the pond, and it was difficult netting them and throwing them back in the lake a block away. Garden snakes were caught and released a block away. Things went well for several years as long as I maintained and cleaned and kept close watch on the pond. The real clincher came as a subtle lure of amusement and excitement. I observed what I thought was two cute little beavers making waves circling round and round in the pond. I didn't think beavers would be harmful to the pond, so I left them alone to frolic in the pond. I noticed the lilies began to dwindle down and the fish began to disappear. I asked a couple of my outdoorsmen friends about beavers, and they both said to me, "Are you sure they are beavers? Sounds more like muskrats to me." They asked me to look at the tails to see if they are paddle shaped or long and black like a rat's tail. They said if it is muskrats, they will destroy the pond. Well they were muskrats, and they ate the lilies down to the roots. They ate the fish and burrowed a subterranean escape route and left the pond desolate.

Unexpected Problems

I did not expect the visitors that came to my pond. I thought I knew enough about water habitats to be completely successful and I was for quite a while, so what went wrong? This thing that scientists conveniently call instinct explains how animals and all living creatures know how to communicate and build habitats, like a spider conveniently spinning this perfect geometrical web without any tools or measurement. How did they know where my pond was, despite the fence and thick shrubs and obstacles hiding it? They just followed the laws of nature, while man makes up his own rules as he goes along.

The *muskrats* were like the killer parasites which looked at and cased a communal host of victims. They just used the host pond and played in it and had fun indulging in every way and then made an escape route to seek and destroy another host pond.

The Human Factor

Nature sometimes takes many years to form its own ecosystem, but man alters it and modifies it and hurries the process and then encounters unforeseen problems. We can create an environment to attract a certain class of people, like a fifty-five plus community that has security. This lowers the probability of crime and undesirable people, but foolproof it is not. Likewise when we relocate to a new community, city, or country, we expose ourselves to the human ecosystem that is in place. It is all about choices and making the difference in an environment to create harmony and coexistence, which we will elaborate on in our next section.

Ecological Transportation

    Different species of animals and organisms depend on other species to generate their presence in a new frontier. Plants and trees are stationary, and the "cause and effect" principle comes into play, to generate their population in other areas and environments. The wind blows the pollen and spores of plants and trees, which in a sense gives them wings to travel. Bees pollinate flowers, which gives the flowers working caretakers. The caretakers' reward is making honey. The sun draws pollen, spores, small animal and insect eggs, and moisture into the atmosphere. It is then caught in the clouds and returns to the earth via rain. It gives me a profound appreciation of the interaction, rhythm, harmony, and pulse of nature playing a masterful symphony of life. It is no doubt intelligent design, but some ignorant scientists want to explain it away as the big bang, or millions of years to develop. Who made the first element? Where did the first seed come from? There are so many questions and new theories, and they are constantly seeking new evidence to support their fractured ideas—all because they could not admit that God *is God* and the only one that can make something from nothing. Some of the really intelligent ones will retort "Well who made God?" Einstein couldn't answer that or how the universe ends. When will man admit that the mysteries of things that exist are beyond our comprehension? All I know is that all the greatest minds in the world put together are like a grain of sand on the ocean floor compared to the Creator.

    I am sorry I got a little carried away, but I am only human. I have limited abilities, and I am living in a world so awesome and complex that I choose to just appreciate it and be fascinated with its glorious design and that I must humbly proclaim "What an awesome God."

Positive and Negative

    Previously we covered "cause and effect." Before we delve into the pros and cons of cause and effect with the human application, we must first look at the parasite and small creatures to get the big picture. I would like to share with you an amazing observation that I and my fellow colleagues witnessed outside of our busy salon in

Woodbury, New Jersey. There was this spider that spun his web outside the window of the salon connecting it between the window sill and an evergreen bush. We watched the spider trap flies and aphids, and he would encase them with his string of web material like he was wrapping his lunch. We would revisit the spider to see his progress, and one of the stylists named Bill was getting bored and decided to have fun with this spider. Bill threw some seeded red pepper on the web. We watched the spider patiently kick off the pepper with his hind legs until it was clear. He proceeded to hide in the bushes waiting for his victims. Bill got bored with that and decided to poke holes in the web. The spider repaired the holes and braced it up with more web support. Bill threw more pepper on the web, and the spider cleaned it up. Bill busted up the web real good the next time, and the spider built a bigger and stronger web. Well the next day, Frank, Fran, Bill, and I went out to check on the spider. As Bill approached closer to the web, the spider noticed him and seemed to position himself in attack mode in the center of the web. At this point, the spider had enough and wasn't going to put up with any more crap. The spider rocked forward and backward on the web like a trampoline and lunged onto Bill's chest and onto the ground and scurried away. Bill got scared, and we all laughed.

Human Application

The positive and negative or cause and effect principle when applied to parasitic people brings about pseudo-similar ways and means of continuing their existence. The host often creates the environment that he or she lives out he or she lives in. Whether intentionally or unintentionally, the element of surprise of cause and effect can play a major role in the outcome. My wife, Delia, loves nature and feeds several feral cats and raccoons that hang around our house. I tried to warn her about feeding them too much. We now have several wildcats and four or five raccoons in our yard most of the time. They fight over superiority. The communication between species is like mixing politics with religion—segregation and separation, driving the wedge of differences between what could have been balanced and mutual cohabitation and also depending on one another in mixed breeds and confusion of choosing sides. Boards and gangs and committees are formed. It is a matter of who's got rights rather than what is right. The truth is that we can't please everybody, but choose what is right. Choose what is best for the whole of society.

In chapter 3, we will cover atmospheric adaptation.

And I will restore to you the years that the locust hath eaten, the cankerworm, and the caterpillar, and the palmerworm, my great army which I sent among you. (Joel 2:25)

Chapter 3

Environmental Adaptation: Production, Entrapment, Privacy, Computer Age

A parasite will do whatever it can to survive. The world is a stage, and they each act their part playing between hosts to interact in their favor. They will pit hosts against one another or join them together, depending on the parasite's needs and reproduction of its species.

In chapter 2, we delved into the evolutionary aspect of parasites and the conditions that best support their continuance.

In this chapter, we are directing your attention to the different methods parasites use. It is just like a Hollywood production where parasites create actors, promoters, scriptwriters, directors, a stage, a scene, a plot, a story line, and a motive. They create a theater of action, suspense, emotions, drama, and even comedy humor at the expense of the host. They can play a number of Oscar-winning roles to win your sympathy and promote their cause.

Production

To produce and reproduce at a rapid rate gives parasites a gaining advantage over the slower-moving host. I remember seeing a cartoon in a magazine that showed Noah's ark, and I saw two giraffes, two lions, two sheep, etc., but a bunch of rabbits. The caption said, "I thought there was only supposed to be two of each kind?" Rabbits reproduce quickly and much more than humans. Yet it is a small illustration of how much faster than rabbits the parasites reproduce.

Dandruff and psoriasis happen in patches due to a high pH level in the skin and scalp.

In my cosmetology training, we learned that the scalp and skin should be pH 4.5 to 5.0 which is a little on the acidic side to discourage bacteria from having a hotbed environment to thrive in. The skin and scalp get red and scaly and itchy and are sore and tender to touch. Most of the time, the condition is due to shampoo, soap, and detergent that are high in pH. It can also come from a poor diet and personal hygiene. I often recommend an acid-balanced shampoo and a soap bar like Dove soap that is not harsh. I also recommend drinking a half-shot glass of apple cider vinegar a day. So just as you have to make sure the pH level is right on your skin and scalp, you have to check the conditions to be parasite free and protected.

Parasitic people look for the kind of environment to adapt to where they can be secure and productive. These players play on your five senses in the material world to cause *host* entrapment.

Entrapment

Most parasites will keep their host alive long enough to complete their cycle. There is of course the "dark horse" or, put in another way, a Darth Vader type of character role. The sole purpose of this kind is to make a total end of the "host," so long as they have another host to jump on to. This type of parasite needs to be eradicated. *Eradicated*, when referring to parasitic people, means that they have to be institutionalized or put in a long-term halfway house or rehab or at least two plus years in prison. If not, they will make an end of you and your species.

The Worst *Parasitic People*

Eradicated is maybe a harsh word to use. Confined, hindered, restrained, repressed, and shut up might better describe or depict what has to be done. These extremely aggressive types deceive while being deceived. They entrap while being entrapped. In their vexation, they terrorize others. In my own life and in the lives of family and friends, I've witnessed many times the parasitic people in and out of court and jail, only to be put back in a population continuing in their debauchery. I sat in court in New Jersey a few hours listening to ninety cases before the judge, of which only three went to jail. The reason the three went to jail was because they refused to pay the fine. Let me see—it comes down to money. The courts rake in thousands of dollars on court costs and fines. They would rather send them out in the street and have them back next month for court and to pay a fine. The court will make the charges seem worse than it is and encourage you to obtain a lawyer, so that they won't have to pay for using a public defender. The host will post bail to get the parasite out, only to do another crime and be back to square one. The host thinks he or she is doing good helping these parasites back on their feet. Truth of the matter is that the host is aiding and abetting. The host is enabling the worst type of parasitic person to continue breaking the law, showing disrespect, defiant, and self-destructive. Their chronic, habitual addictions and unfavorable outlook on life will make the host's life and those of closely associated with the host most troubled and sear in misery. There is only one way to deal with this tragic circumstance: That is tough love.

Tough Love

As parents, this is the hardest thing to face, especially when a parent loves their son or daughter so much that they sacrificially made it so convenient for them that they made little or no effort to struggle on their own. As a parent, we have a natural tendency to want our children to have more than what we had. The old saying "No pain, no gain" is quite true in many cases. When we make an effort to accomplish, we receive somewhat of a reward. There is less appreciation for something given to us than something that we worked for. Given as a gift, a necessity, or something you desired that you could not afford may be an exception to the rule.

Tough love is no guarantee that the results will be favorable. The ultimate sacrifice may be death to the host or parasitic person.

PARASITIC PEOPLE

As a Christian, I lean heavily on trusting God. I admit that there are many times I have an argument with God. He always wins the argument, but in all fairness, his ways are above my ways and his thoughts above my thoughts. Strangely enough, when I lose, I win!!! I deserved to lose because I doubted God. Even for a moment of doubt, you can sink below the waves. This was illustrated when Peter bid Jesus to meet him on the water. Peter stepped off the boat and began to walk on the water toward Jesus. Somewhere between hearing and seeing the roar of the wind and the waves crashing, Peter doubted for a moment and suddenly began to sink below the waves. Jesus lifted him out and accompanied him back to the safety of the boat.

Humility

I go through some really tough times in my life. Sometimes I go to bed wondering if I will get a good night's sleep. This much I do know. I always have food in the fridge, a roof over my head, and a grateful heart that I have another day of life to experience. I feel so unworthy and spoiled when I complain about my problems. My sister Margie lost a son. Her daughter Kim lost three daughters. The faith and strength they both have in the most heartrending circumstances makes me feel ashamed of myself for complaining. Lots of times, we reflect back and entertain the "Shouda, woulda, coulda" concept. Yes, hind sight is twenty-twenty, but we need to see what we can do in our present state and steps we can take to secure our future. Then there is the blame game, and we have "to whom the fault falls" on.

Psychology Today

I gave up on the psychology they employ today, to explain away what they don't understand. They blame somebody or something else for the deep-seated problems an individual is having. I watched a TV program where a panel of these so-called experts was analogizing a serial killer. I don't recall the number of people this man killed, but the panel of experts concluded that when he was twelve years old, his mother slapped him in the face in front of his friends and he lost his self-esteem. What? You mean to say that it was the mother's fault for him killing all those people? How does that rest with you? Should we put the mother in prison and the young confused man in anger management? Truth is that we don't know what trips off a mind. We can change our minds, get overexcited, be tense, be complacent, and change the outcome.

The mind is so complex and, when exposed to certain environments, conditions, and forms of stimuli, unique and personalized, will respond. So how do we deal with parasitic people who are unstable and have a distorted view of life? No answer I give you is 100%. However, we can increase our chances of success by applying *love*—not as in giving them what they want but by pointing them in the direction of what they need. "Love wins." Be wise in saying "yes" to that which you perceive to be good for the person. Be extremely wise in saying "no" when you sense danger or a red flag. Tough love again enters at a time, where the host thinks the parasite hopefully would change, maybe in a life-threatening situation. They may threaten suicide and play on the host's emotions. Call it a gamble, or a chance, but one thing is for sure: If nothing is done, the situation will get increasingly worse, for both the host and the parasitic person. Early detection and prevention is the first and foremost best thing you can do. The longer the host allows the transgressor to transgress, the more difficult the problem becomes. The host will get no respect, no help, no mercy, and no peace.

Privacy and Self-Preservation

We live in an age where privacy is compromised. Also protection and security is stressed with your home, car, and computer. Remember when we talked about the aggressive viral strains that mutate to survive, such as flu vaccines altered each year? Well now we have the cyber parasites who can cleverly clean out your bank account with the use of a computer. We will cover the privacy part first.

Privacy

Technology works for and against us. There are various types of security systems to secure your identity, computer, car, home, and business. At the same time, the parasitic people have an eye on you through computers, cell phones, and now drones. Our privacy has been so compromised through the use of bar codes and phones. Any of your membership and credit cards or supermarket cards keep track of all your transactions. The supermarket even knows what brand of toilet paper you buy! Whether it is a cell phone or land line phone, they log even local calls on the mainframe and sell the information to local businesses to seek your patronage. That is to say, you call your favorite pizza shop every Friday night for pickup or delivery. Another pizza shop moves into the area and buys a list off the phone company to send you coupons in the mail, say 20 to 50 percent off your first order. You think that everybody got that in their mail, but in truth you were not chosen randomly.

Computer Age

We are living in a computer age where much of our personal information is accessible. Hackers are parasitic people positioned into place to give you a virus. Some extort by sending you an encrypted message to pay them several hundred dollars, or else your computer will shut down losing all your data. Intelligent criminals are the worst parasites. They are opportunists waiting for the precise moment to wreak havoc on your life.

On Facebook, they know whom your friends are, your likes and dislikes, and your praises and complaints. They know your political affiliation, your faith, your ambitions, and what makes you happy and sad. They know if you are married or single or have children. They know where you live and what you do. Unless you are Amish or a homeless person, they pretty much know where to find you. This is the reality of the world we live in.

Unless your head is above the clouds, you will be under the weather with the rest of us. A possible safeguard and solution would be to keep sober, be vigilant, and keep your guard up. Be careful what you say or do in public or cyberspace. Put your trust in God, not in man. If you have doubts, don't even trust yourself. Self-preservation is not to be confused with selfishness. Self-preservation comes with self-respect; and self-respect reflects and reveals your attitude in dealing with others.

I remember hearing an evangelist as he motioned with his hand up and down and horizontally left to right in the form of a cross saying, "Your vertical relationship between you and God reflects your horizontal relationship with others."

Chapter 4

Parasitic Personality: Characteristics, Profile, Addictions

What Is Not Parasitic

It is not always a lazy person, an unmotivated person, or a depressed person. It is not someone stressed out, nonsocial, mean, or pesty. These are certainly not good traits in a person, but they not necessarily make for a parasitic person.

Parasitic Characteristics

Now the following habits or manner that parasitic people characterize will have some and possibly all of the following traits. Some may show the early signs of parasitic behavior and may change for the better and avoid a life of turmoil.

Entertainment

They get bored easily and need constant stimuli. They never allow quiet time to reflect or meditate. They clutter their mind with senseless trivia and nonsense.

Noise

They usually talk loud and play loud rap or hip-hop music—often music with an anti-establishment protest flavor. It is as if they are trying to stifle anything entering their head.

No Conscience

They put on like they are concerned, but they are actors as I mentioned previously. They are self-willed, and on the surface they act concerned, but they really don't care. It is a selfish lifestyle that proclaims "What's in it for me?" Almost all the people they befriend are a host in some way. Every host is going to satisfy the parasitic person (i.e., drugs, sex, good times, shelter, entertainment, or food).

> *And herein do I exercise myself, to have always a conscience void of offense toward God and toward men.* (Acts 24:16)

No Attention Span

As mentioned before about clutter, this becomes the reason for lack of attention. I have witnessed a number of parasitic people whose attention span is only about four or five minutes long. It would not be good for maintaining a job. They will stop and smoke a cigarette or get a drink or spend time in the bathroom.

Poor Outlook

The parasitic person usually has a poor outlook on life. Often it stems from a bad childhood. It is like an alcoholic's excuse: "I am what I am because_____." You fill in the blanks. They feel sorry for themselves and blame it on other circumstances or people. They are insecure but act as if they are confident. They feel cheated in the game of life and want to take it back at all cost to themselves and others. The average person would be happy for family or close friends who landed a good job or received an achievement award. The parasitic would cry out injustice and say, "Why did he or she get that? It is unfair. I should have gotten it." Jealousy is to the core.

Worthless Conversation

I know that sounds terrible, but it is a fact that they talk gibberish like a drunk in barroom chatter. They also talk to themselves (the only one who gives them undivided attention).

> *For out of the abundance of the heart the mouth speaketh.* (Matthew 12:34b)

In other words, what they are speaking comes from their heart, and what you hear as a host is an abundance of lies or deception.

Excessive

Parasitic people are extreme and without composure. They are compulsive and undisciplined. They even eat compulsively. They are wired up and get little sleep. As I mentioned earlier, they pass out and suddenly come to.

Children of the Night

They are mostly nocturnal creatures that prowl the night. Their naps would be mostly daytime. Even though they will exhibit foul deeds in broad daylight for shock value, they prefer the cover of night to be sneaky.

Handouts

They constantly look for host handouts—free food, next to nothing place to stay, and use of utilities to excess. They are reluctant to work it off and make excuses to bail out. Now when people are poor and have hungry mouths to feed, this makes an exception to this rule. Hardships fall on people at times with unforeseeable circumstances beyond their control. These folks are not parasitic people, and Christian compassion should be exercised.

No Meaningful Interests

There are no hobbies or talents to occupy their mind. There is no reading a book or getting involved in help groups.

Violent Mood Swings

It is like a freight train passing through their heads. Unable to stop, they carry a load of junk through the crossroads. Frustration and confusion trips the circuit and puts them out of control—moody.

Greedy

Now there are many especially here in the USA that are greedy—greedy businesses, bosses, coworkers, and those of family and friends.

So that is not the same kind of greed that a parasitic person has. The difference is that the greedy people mentioned above work hard, connive, push their way groping to the top, and even kill if necessary to achieve their goal. That sounds pretty bad, but at least they do everything they can to get there. Now the parasitic person differs in the sense that they just takes, not achieves. They are tightfisted and ravenously devour their host. They are military strategists and use first strike advantage to conquer the host, who is surprised and unaware of his or her demise. They take by deception.

Causes Division

Parasitic people are masters of creating differences between host species. If they feel the threat of other people influencing their intended host, they will try to separate or destroy the intruders. They will pit husbands and wives against each other. They will point out differences to cause division, that is, the color of your skin or your political preferences. They will mock the intruder's character and intentions to create an atmosphere of resentment between the host and so-called or implied intruder. They will convince the host that they are saving or rescuing the host from intruders. Once the parasitic person eliminates or reduces the threat of intruders, they will then hanker down in complete confidence.

Addictions

Parasitic people are addictive people. They pop pills and drink booze to the point where they are senseless. The real world hurts too much, so they want to drown in their sorrows. The sad part about it is that nowadays $10.00 is all you need to get stoned for the day. It will buy you heroin, pot meth, alcohol, and cocaine. Yep, get high pretty cheap. Now if you do a little math and add another $6.00 for cigarettes, that would make it $16.00 a day. In a month, it comes to nearly $500.00. That is money that could have gone toward rent, a mortgage, or a luxury car payment.

Listen. If the parasitic is on drugs and/or alcohol and has close relations to the host, the host will experience hell on the earth. Just giving them a few bucks will make the host an enabler. I am so guilty of this, and I am so remorseful. With good intentions, I was actually aiding and abetting a bad vice. I recall a man who was the town alcoholic, and he would do odd jobs to get paid in mostly a bottle of liquor. He came into my salon one day asking me for money to buy lunch. There was Burger King across the street, and next to it was a liquor store. I will call him Henry. I gave Henry $7.00 and said to him, "I am watching you cross the street, and I better see you go into Burger King and not the liquor store, or I won't give you money anymore." Sure enough he went into Burger King, but I saw him sneak out the side door into the liquor store. He came the next day asking money for food, and I confronted him about the day before and refused him money. He yelled, "I will see you in *hell*!!!" The next day he was run over killed by a truck.

Gangland Style

Parasitic people cause division between the host and their company of people, but remember parasites stick together to create an environment for them to increase in numbers. They have a code of honor so to speak, where they have common interests to maintain their stability. Even though parasitic people are selfish and greedy and nonsocialites, they rely on their gang of parasites to help them in time of wants (not needs). They seek connections for food, drugs, shelter, and entertainment. They will case the area and get familiar with transportation, hot spots, and places to do their business. They will identify with like-minded parasitic people and give each other approval with a sly look or give each other a high five.

No Self-Worth

Parasitic people have a low self-esteem and look at others who are successful in life with loathing. This is probably a key factor that drives the parasitic person into bad behavior. They look at themselves with pity and feel that they have been shunned by society. They think that circumstance brought them to this, and because they have been victimized, they want to punish society.

In the next chapter, we will look into the possible reasons parasitic people became that way. We will cover preventive measures that might spare the host of problems. We will talk about recovery programs and help groups. Be positive and say that with every problem there is a solution.

> *O Israel, thou hast destroyed thyself; but in me is thine help.* (Hosea 13:9)

CHAPTER 5

How Parasitic People Got That Way: The Beginning, Identity Crisis, Feeding the Flesh, Can't Talk to God, Family

The Beginning

In rare cases there could be a birth defect (i.e., genetic disease, AIDS), when born to alcoholic or drug-addicted parents. Being careless or abusive with drugs and smoking especially for pregnant mothers will result in defective births. When in office, President Ronald Reagan was confronted with the AIDS crisis and what role the government would play to fix this epidemic. He said, "It is a behavioral problem." Now that did not float well with some people, but when you look at the facts, it holds true. The majority of AIDS victims are among homosexual males engaging in anal intercourse. Heterosexual multipartner relationships are also plagued with venereal disease (VD) and other sexually transmitted diseases. When parents are addicted to drugs, alcohol, and cigarettes especially pregnant females, they run the risk of premature birth and genetically defective babies. I said all that to say this: It may be a valid reason a person becomes parasitic in such circumstances. However, the behavioral aspect still is a matter of self-willed choices. In the history books, you will find many famous people who became overcomers and achievers, despite their handicaps, who defied the odds stacked up against them. My wife, Delia, was born hard of hearing and became mentally deficient from not learning at a normal hearing level. Her mother had German measles when carrying Delia in pregnancy, and doctors said that was the reason for the birth defect. Now her other senses became sharper than the average person. Her sense of smell is like a blood hound. We were in the third floor attic of her house, and she said to me that somebody came in through the back door. She felt the vibration. Delia got certified in cosmetology and massage therapy. She worked hard and beat the odds, of which I am proud.

Traumatized Childhood

This is perhaps the most horrible possibility why parasitic people got that way. As a Christian counselor, I have both heard and witnessed the most deplorable conditions in which a child was raised.

I and my two older sisters agree that we had the most wonderful dad and mom in the whole world. We got scolded, punished, and hit when we were disrespectful and disobedient. Now maybe today's standard labels parents "abusive" if they strike a child, but it is certainly not the case with our parents.

There is a song entitled "Daddy's Hand" that sort of told it like it is: Daddy's hand would comfort and cuddle. Daddy's hand would spank, when it was necessary, *but* always with *love* unfeigned.

I had to say that, because I had a wonderful childhood. I am not going to lie to you, saying that I know what less fortunate people have gone through nor how they felt in a less favorable environment. However, I did have to try to piece together broken families, blended families with stepsiblings, and troubled, strained relationships. It is only my being sensitive to the leading of the heavenly Father, his Holy Spirit, and the mercy and grace of our Lord and Savior Jesus Christ that gave me wisdom and direction in dealing with the problems that beset so many people.

When you feel like you are losing everything, that is when you cling to that which you have now with more appreciation.

> *The righteousness of the perfect shall direct his way: but the wicked shall fall by his own wickedness.* (Proverbs 11:5)

PARASITIC PEOPLE

The rod and reproof give wisdom: but a child left to himself bringeth his mother to shame. When the wicked are multiplied, transgression increaseth: but the righteous shall see their fall. Correct thy son, and he shall give thee rest; yea, he shall give delight unto thy soul. (Proverbs 29:17–17)

Now I am not going to say, "Do as I say, not as I do." I went through a bitter and sad divorce. Before I knew the Lord, I made some tragic mistakes. Even after I came to know the Lord, I made bad decisions that by the grace of God only was I spared dire consequences. The mother of my two daughters who is now deceased had custody of them. I am not going to criticize my ex-wife, because she is not here to defend herself. My children grew up in a far less than perfect environment. They both grew up experiencing the most hellish conditions. My heart ached as I witnessed them struggling through their adulthood. Even though I helped them with their financial needs, the hauntings of the past vexed them. To make a long story short, they both have learned, with myself included, that life is a roller-coaster experience. Despite the ups and more frequent downs, we found that the grace of God sustained us. The hope for the future is greater than the torment of the past. Even now, with a less than perfect life in an imperfect world and my daughters who are now mothers and grandmothers, through it all, living in a world of darkness, God shines his light. I would not trade my girls for anybody else. They might have wanted to trade me, but they are stuck with me. God has strange humor at times, but trusting him is wise.

When there is not the traditional family consisting of the original mother and father together, there will be problems. Some of these problems are seemingly unsurmountable, especially to a young child who doesn't understand complicated adult differences. A child becomes the victim of adults and the difficulty of choosing sides. A child becomes confused and left with many questions of how and why things are what they are. They end up more often with the greater hurt.

Drug and alcohol abuse witnessed by a young mind will have a profound effect that will shape the rest of their lives. I have heard of a young mother hiding her baby in a laundry basket from being sold by the father for drugs. I heard of a father committing suicide after raping his prepubescent daughter. Countless horror stories from so many people are much too overwhelming to mention in this book.

So where am I going with this? If you are one of those that put a fine line between host and parasite and if grave mistakes were made on both ends, I would urge you to seek counseling. Get involved in help groups. You can't change the past, but you can change the present. I heard this saying that the reason right now is called the present is because it is a gift. That is a good way of looking at it. It is a gift you can open up and explore what is inside. What you do today will shape your tomorrows. Repent of past mistakes and forgive yourself so you can forgive others. Seek God's grace. It is not a matter of whether life is fair or not; it is how you fair life. I have witnessed glorious changes in people's lives. Be one of them.

Identity Crisis

Now that we have covered birth to early childhood years, we will move on to teen and adult years of parasitic people.

From the beginning to the adolescent years, if they were the victims, then the teen years could really mess lives up. Depending on the parent they model themselves with is how the personality is formed. Let us say that the parasitic person saw the mistakes of the bad parent or parents and turned away wisely. You would think that if kids saw what drugs did to their parents, they would have enough sense to steer clear of drugs. *Well,* wrong. They fall into the same trap and even worse. Can't figure it out? Join the crowd; I don't have the answer. However, we can start out new and start out fresh. Nahhh, that ain't gonna work. I told ya. I didn't have the answer, but I know who does.

> *Therefore if any man be in Christ, he is a new creature: old things are passed away; behold, all things have become new.* (2 Corinthians 5:17)

In other words, the power has to come from outside ourselves. In the twelve-step AA program, they say the same thing. God is generalized, but nevertheless one has to seek a spiritual power that elevates the host and the parasitic person to a level of understanding. They have a lost identity crisis, because they cleave to friends having a similar set of circumstances. The hope is that the host they are close to has this connection to that higher power.

Here is the real clincher: The parasitic person has this low self-image. This is for the most part not having respect for themselves. When the stinking thinking increases, the love diminishes both for self and others. The animal instinct to survive takes precedence over sound reasoning. The short-term gratification is their quick fix to a problem. The problem then transfers to the host. Now the disrespect that they have for themselves is projected onto the host. They will convince their host that it is the host's fault and the host needs to make it up to the parasite, as part of their punishment and obligation.

Feeding the Flesh

Parasitic people will constantly feed the flesh. They are excessive eaters if the host invites them to the table or raid the fridge. The funny thing about it is that most of them don't usually have a weight problem. It must be the lack of sleep and on the go constantly that make them that way. And as what I mentioned before, cigarettes, drugs, and alcohol dull their anxiety and help them calm down, or so they think. In actuality, it enrages them more; and if the host supplies them, they just write a death wish. Sex is another avenue they choose to corrupt. It is not love, but rather performance. It is not a means of peace and harmony, but a commodity by which you either make money or gain some kind of access. When they feel unloved, they express it in how they treat others.

They will mark their bodies with piercings and tattoos. It is their way of making a statement to the world. Now don't get me wrong. I am not saying if you smoke and/or have tattoos on your body, you are a parasite. I am saying that in many cases, parasitic people have that characteristic.

Feeding the flesh instead of the spirit is the sum total of slop in, slop out. There is a lack of wholesomeness and interest. With the exception of wanting to look sensual and seductive or brazen and macho, parasitic people will neglect their health. They will push their bodies to the max of abuse. They will drink or drug the hurt or discomfort away, instead of nursing themselves back to health.

The Family Unit

Now here is a tragic epitaph for today's American family. Satan's greatest work is to destroy the family unit. With the divorce rate of first-time marriages now at 50 percent, second-time marriages are even worse at 70 percent. Are you ready for this? Third-time marriages end at 90 percent!!! You would think that the second or third time around would be wiser and treated more carefully and respectfully. Human nature comes into play here. You see we become less tolerant, less patient, more frustrated, and more angry. Whatever went wrong with the first marriage is carried into the second and third. Don't forget the excess baggage (kids), in-laws, and blended stepsons and stepdaughters that have different interests and are from different environments. Resentment and animosity, hatred, and jealousy are rampant. Going back thousands of years, mothers would never leave their children. It wasn't until the last half of the twentieth century that women would leave their children for a carefree life. On a Monday following Mother's Day 2015, I was shocked to hear in the news that a survey was taken in every country of the world to see who were the best mothers. USA came in at thirty-third! If you are a mother and feel offended by that statistics, I will have to say, "My most humble apologies." Especially if you have children that you are proud of, keep doing what you are doing, and God bless you. Statistics apply to those who wanted more out of life, not seeing the needs.

The family unit is more of a concern to the host than the parasitic person in the general sense, unless the host is responsible for the downfall of the parasite. I cannot put everything in a category and expect you to understand what I don't understand. My most fervent prayer is that you rightly divide the truth as I always try to do. I have no formulas, and I learn from experience. In all honesty, I must confess that I had many restless, sleepless nights where I tossed and turned trying to figure things out. It is hard to let go and let God.

Many times I argue with God and scold him for making my life difficult. I try to reason with him and complain that he should test somebody else and stop picking on me all the time. Then I quote his word where he declares that he won't give us any more than we can handle. It comes down to the fact that I am not applying my trust in the Lord. What I am actually saying is, "Please, God, make a liar out of me. Please make me feel ashamed of myself, when you answer my prayers." When he does see me through it all, I am so glad he made me feel foolish. I leap for joy and apologize to the Lord for not putting full trust in him. I just love it and feel so relieved when he proves me wrong. I said all this because I am showing an example of how I rely on the family of God and God as my family.

The parasitic person chooses what he wants as a family. Often it is for selfish gain why parasites grope for meaning and a false sense of security. I honestly can't imagine my life without God, when his awesomeness pulls me out of sinking sand and places my feet on solid ground.

My father was the one who always wanted to get the whole family together. Today, families are pretty spread out over the country. When I was growing up, our relatives were fairly close. Most were in the tri-state area. More specifically Philadelphia, north Delaware, and south New Jersey were the hub of our family get-togethers. My mom had three brothers, and my dad would coax her to invite all three and spouses and children over our house for food and drink. There was a lot of talk and laughter and respect. I remember wholesome upbringing. Yet in spite of the love and values the family embraced and portrayed, parasitic people developed within it. So you see it is not always bad, broken, distressed unloving families that produce parasites. Most often these loving, close families suffer more, because they can't understand what went wrong. In my family, many have moved to Florida—a very big state. However, we manage to be within a 3-hour ride. I take after my father in that I am always trying to get my now elderly sisters, cousins, and uncles together. It took a small miracle to get my two remaining uncles together a couple of years ago, and it was a good thing, because my uncle John passed away less than a year later. I have been trying to get my last remaining uncle, Al, together with my oldest sister, Anna, both in poor health.

None of us are exempt from sickness, tragedy, and death.

> *That ye may be the children of your Father which is in heaven: for He maketh His sun to rise on the evil and the good, and sendeth rain on the just and on the unjust.* (Matthew 5:45)

Family values are only as good as the people who practice it. If you don't think highly of yourself, how could you convince others? Self-preservation comes with self-respect, and self-respect reflects and reveals your attitude in dealing with others. It is easy to love that which belongs to you and brings you pride and joy. To love the unlovable is the hardest thing. However, when it bares fruit, it is worth all the pain and suffering, beholding the glory that follows. I heard a story about a counselor leading a young teen group in Christian values. A teen boy stood up and said to the counselor, "I can't believe what you are saying, because I can't believe what you do." *Wow!* That is sobering to say the least. If you fail to set an example of what is the good and right thing to do, you will fail to reach the unlovable. Parasitic people watch every move their intended host is doing. They are very observant and are opportunists. After careful consideration, they make their move. The host often is unaware of the trap set before them. You quickly become the family host that is going to provide the parasite with all its needs.

All this seems futile. Why does life have to be so complicated? Let me say this to you: When life seems futile, remember the people whose lives you influenced; then you will remember your purpose of being here.

A couple of years ago, I had a Bible study group. I always had it as an open forum for interaction.

In the study group, I brought up a hypothetical question: "Imagine if you will that you have a time machine. Imagine being able to go back in time to the point where you thought you may have skewed off. If you have this chance, what would you change? What would you do differently?"

PARASITIC PEOPLE

Well I heard the usual response I was expecting, like "I would not have married that one," "I would have picked a different occupation," "I wouldn't have lived in that area," "I would have continued my education," etc.

Then at the end of the line, it was my turn. I simply said, "I wouldn't change a thing." A fellow member, Gordon, blurted out in a haughty but joking way, "Why is that, Pastor Ron? Because you did everything right?" I answered, "No, not at all. In fact, I probably did more wrong than all of you put together. However, it brought me to the place where I am now. Praise be to God. That means all the bad decisions, mistakes, and choices in life led me to the place I am right now. In fact, we would not be having a Bible study right now."

And we know that all things work together for good to them that love God, to them who are called according to his purpose. (Romans 8:28)

You cannot mend that which is not broken. Only in brokenness can the healing begin.

Life is not a handout. It is something you chase after, with all your heart, mind, and soul.

Let us move on to the next level.

Can't Talk to God

Some parasitic people think they are talking to God, when actually they are talking to demons. Now prepare yourselves, because this subject matter is very hard to ingest. I am not laying Hollywood glitz on you and trying to sensationalize this controversial outlook on the inner workings of the dark side. It is necessary to help you understand how darkness enters an individual. I am not saying all parasitic people are demon possessed. However, there are signs to look for that would help you identify the evil source.

We covered the traits of the parasitic person as far as filling their lives with noise and clutter. They don't leave any room for the small voice within to comfort them and lead them. Because their house is left desolate and wanting, they become restless and bored. Because of the noise, they can't hear God. Sometimes God has to first get our attention. It reminds me of a joke I heard about a man. He went to a farm and noticed the donkey working hard for the farmer. The farmer pulled on the straps, and the donkey pulled a wagon of timbers to a spot where the farmer pointed to and stopped. The man was so impressed that he offered the farmer a lot of money to take the donkey home. The farmer agreed on the price, and the man took the donkey home. When he unloaded the donkey from the truck, the donkey just stood there. The man pushed and pulled at the beast to no avail. Finally he managed to force the beast back into the truck and drove back to the farmer. The man said to the farmer, "I tried to get the donkey to move and he does nothing! I don't understand. He worked hard for you." Just then the farmer said "excuse me" and went behind the barn. The farmer came out from behind the barn with a piece of 2 × 4 lumber. He walked up to the donkey and wacked him in the head. Suddenly the donkey started moving. The farmer said to the man, "You see you got to get his attention first." Likewise, in a spiritual sense, we need to be wacked upside the head to wake up and pay attention. With sad circumstances and situations, we suddenly realize, often too late, that we were wrong in the way we went about it. Trouble drives many to peril. Trouble drove me to God.

When one is in the valley is when that one hears from God. That is where one learns a lesson and helps that one reach higher ground.

And because iniquity shall abound, the love of many shall wax cold. (Matthew 24:12)

Is it me or does it seem to be more sin in the world? Parasitic people wax cold because the love is lacking in their lives. The host extends help in loving kindness and gets caught in the spider's web. How do we know when to step back or move forward with helping parasites?

I have had my fair share of parasitic people, maybe more than most hosts. So my suggestions and recommendations come from the proverbial school of hard knocks.

PARASITIC PEOPLE

But the hour cometh and now is, when the true worshipers shall worship the Father in spirit and in truth: for the Father seeketh such to worship Him. (John 4:23)

In the late 1960s, I was very bad. I was never hooked on drugs, but I sampled anything sent my way. It wasn't until I almost totaled myself on lysergic acid diethylamide (LSD) that I sought God.

Sometimes we have to bottom out before we see God and talk to him. In my experience it came down to realizing that if I were to continue in this destructive mode, I would probably die. It is at this point of realization that we come to terms and realize that "Yes, there is a problem." If parasitic people deny that they have a problem, then there is no place for cure or allowing God in. When God is locked out, the devil steps in and makes a few changes.

Indirectly the devil influences your decision. Directly your will enforces it. By invitation, the Lord fixes it.

When you allow the parasitic person in your life, you have to count the cost. You may be able to lead them on the path of righteous living, or you just might make them worse. When saying *no* to them hurts, it is because you as the host know that patronizing them would mean a continuation of their fractured lifestyle.

Tough Love

Yes, you take the chance of losing them. However, you would lose them anyhow and probably more tragically. They threaten suicide and harm to themselves and others. Here is where trust in God comes in. I once even vomited saying *no*, but my trust in Jesus was fruitful. Let God deal with them.

Chapter 6

Demons and Angels

Demon Possession

Early in the fifth chapter, I mentioned this disturbing possibility of possession. *Mark 5:1–13* is the story of the Gadarene maniac. It was a man who lived among the tombs. Nobody was able to bind him. He even broke chains. "What have I to do with thee, Jesus, thou Son of the most high God? I adjure thee by God, that thou torment me not." Now here is a man with a legion (many) demons who recognized whom Jesus was, and the religious Pharisees and Sadducees did not recognize him. When Jesus was about to cast out the demons, they besought him saying, "Send us into the swine, that we may enter into them." (This is because demons must have a body or host to enter into.) Jesus sent the demons into two thousand swine: and the herd ran violently down a steep place and choked themselves in the sea.

Now isn't it amazing how one man carried a legion of demons for a long time and two thousand pigs couldn't stand having them for a moment? Jesus did warn us to be aware that a man does not deceive us. What the Lord is saying here is that demons are in chains according to the book of *Jude*. It tells how these wicked spirits are limited in what they can do because they are bound in darkness. That is, a demon cannot rape a woman against her will. A human sure can. Imagine a ferocious dog on a chain. You might get away with teasing the dog as long as you are outside the circle limit of the chain. If you tease him right on the line, you will get a little torn up. You step inside that circle, and you get mangled or even killed. So demon spirits can bluff you, tempt you, influence you, and even give you what you wanted. Your *will* is the only defense you have against these seducing spirits.

Put in another way, demon-possessed people are more dangerous than just demons alone. Possession only comes when a person willfully allows seducing evil spirits into their lives. A problem increases if the demon spirit brings others. Demons are parasitic also.

I am going to lay some heavy stuff on you. I am giving you the bad news first. I promise you that afterward I will give you the good news which will far outweigh the bad. It is necessary to understand the enemy. Never underestimate the enemy. Remember Satan has been around a long time. I have a saying, "Temptation is distraction pondered." The devil is good at distracting. I'm sure you've seen commercials about texting and driving—more deadly than drunk driving. Every day we are distracted and deceived—telemarketers, bills, things broken, and feeling tired and/or sick. All that happens without the help of demons. I brought it up because the world we live in can be quite hostile at times. However, it is the way we handle it that makes the difference. So now that we know demons are limited in what they can do, our focus should be on how we avoid them and also how to keep them from parasitic people. If you are a victimized host, you might say to me, "Well, Ron, you don't know what I am going through." Maybe not. However, if you are passing through it, you'll reach the other side.

Telltales of Demon Possession

If you are strong in your Christian faith, a demon-possessed person cannot look you in the eyes. They will look away from direct contact with your eyes, especially if they are lying. They will flail their hands and mumble, often talking to themselves. Their back is hunched between their shoulders and their head protruding forward. They have no repentance or remorse for what they do wrong. They have a mind void of conscience. They may apologize, and seem sorry, but it is always a front. You see they have to protect their access to the host. All the prisoners say they are innocent.

My advice to you is to avoid the demon-possessed parasitic person. They will make life hell for you. I mean that literally. If it is a relative or close friend, you are going to need a lot of prayer and outside help. You cannot, and I repeat, *cannot*, handle someone like that on your own.

> *A prophet is not without honor, save (except) in his own country, and in his own house.* (Matthew 13:57b)

Don't play King David against Goliath. In the book of *Acts 19:13–20*, read about the seven sons of Sceva, who were trying to cast out demons without a heartfelt faith in Jesus Christ. The evil spirits overcame them, and they ran away naked and wounded.

I don't care what church you are from, keep in mind the power of the Holy Spirit must be in operation to win over the forces of darkness. If you have your doubts, stay away from exorcism.

> *And these signs shall follow them that believe; In my name (Jesus) shall they cast out devils; they shall speak with new tongues. They shall take up serpents; and if they drink any deadly thing, it shall not hurt them; they shall lay hands on the sick, and they shall recover.* (Mark 16:17, 17)

Demon Limitations

In addition to reading the book of *Jude* about demon limitations, also read some of these other scriptures that I marked with a subject heading:

- I never knew you . . . (Matthew 7:12)
- Cast out with the Word . . . (Matthew 8:16)
- Be sober, be vigilant . . . (1 Peter 5:8)
- Satan as lightning, power to tread . . . (Luke 10:18, 19)

So now that we know that demons are subjected to the Holy Spirit in the name of Jesus, and we know that we are victorious and conquerors over the works of darkness, let's move on to the next phase.

Demon Influence

When parasitic people allow seducing evil spirits in, it is the beginning of sorrows. Yes, our will and our will alone makes all the difference. When going to places where one knows are a dark snake pit, one invites trouble. If you stop feeding the parasitic person, they will find their feeding ground. Try to steer them away from other parasites that are evil in their thinking. Be persistent in emulating good habits and values. Don't allow loud rebellious music and violent dark programs on the TV or computer. Try to get them interested in good pastime crafts or hobby. If all these fail, then *kick them out*!!! You will save your life and maybe force the parasitic person with demon spirits to seek help.

Demon Friends

In the beginning chapters, there was an overview of parasite habitat and environment. When the environment is suitable to the parasite, many more evolve. Parasitic people choose friends that share similar interests. Demon-possessed parasites will hamper the parasitic person the host is trying to save. That is, if they end up in jail, they learn a few more tricks during their stay.

Demon Connections

Now the parasitic person has a valuable connection to these dark spirits. That is why repeat offenses end them up repeatedly in jail or against the law. Remember how I said that they increase in numbers and strength while the host grows weaker? Such is the case especially with demon-possessed parasites.

Poor Host

Just another seemingly insurmountable mountain to cross, the only thing a host can do is try to isolate and detach them from the influence of other parasitic people. Unless you have a lot of money, you won't be able to be effective in getting them involved in a rehab program. Unfortunately, even a lot of church-based non-profit organizations have operational costs above and beyond the donations. A little homework might prove effective. Ask around and open up to people you could trust, and you might be surprised to find that your problem is not so unique, not so uncommon.

> *Brethren, if a man be overtaken in a fault, ye which are spiritual, restore such a one in the spirit of meekness; considering thyself, lest thou also be tempted. Bear ye one another's burdens, and so fulfil the law of Christ.* (Galatians 6:1, 2)

Accuser of the Brethren

This was the title or name given to Satan in *Revelation 12:10*. The demonized parasitic person will blackmail the host before all the families and friends and will make outright lies and accusations to mare the integrity or credibility of the host. This is the way they justify their evil, wicked ways. They really think they are the victims and that the host should repent and give them a place in their lives. These parasites will put the guilt and blame on everybody but themselves. They will deny that they have a problem. They will say that they have control, when the truth is they have no self-control or discipline.

Fallen Angels

Remember these spirits that take control of parasitic people are angelic beings. One-third of them fell from heaven with Satan to the earth. That could be millions or maybe even billions of wicked spirits roaming through the earth. The description of angels range from tiny to man-size to as tall as skyscrapers. We are in this body of flesh and we are three dimensional. We have a solid form, and we can't pass through walls without getting seriously hurt. I don't think they can feel hot and cold to touch like us nor use the five senses in the same way we do. The reason I say that is because demon spirits need a body to inhabit so they can feel the sensation of flesh. And for this reason, they don't want to vacate.

Angels

Enough about wicked spirits. I did promise you that I would tell you the bad news first and then I would tell you the good news. That means two-thirds of the spirit beings are with God. And, if they are with God, then they are there to serve and protect you. Isn't that neat when you think about it? When I was in a mess of trouble with demon activity, I have to say that I believe that I had three guardian angels protecting me.

In fact the testimonials of my life and experience with angelic intervention would take up the next chapter. Some of the inspiring testimonies of others will be included. Chapter 7 will give the host a break from the heavy-duty stress I might have inflicted on. Do bear in mind that it was the frontline experience I had with parasitic people and/or demon-possessed people that prompted me to write this book. Yes, I am acquainted with sorrow. Yes, I have gone through it. Yes, I wised up the hard way. My stupidity and lack of wisdom should have finished me off. It was the grace of God that saved me and planted my feet on solid ground. It was the intervention of angelic hosts that kept me from destruction. So be prepared to be lifted up with the angels and share with me the heavenly experience. If God could love a sinner like me, you are no exception to the rule.

Chapter 7

Angels to the Rescue

The Strawberry Patch

In my early Christian years following my hippie smoke head era, things were happening to me as a new believer. I felt the safety and security of the Holy Spirit, like a baby eaglet high in the rocky mountain in the fine downy feathers lining the nest, awaiting Mom to bring me my food. Okay, maybe I am getting a little too dramatic. My point is that as a new believer, we seem to have more of a childlike trust that God will protect us. It seemed that as I got more mature in my faith walk, I got less trusting and let doubt creep in. Jesus alluded to this childlike trust in God, like we would trust our parents growing up.

Anyhow, my experience in these early years brought me back to the place when I first believed. Let us never grow dim in our faith and expect a miracle at any time.

In the early 1970s, I had a red 1964 Ford Galaxie Convertible. In Deptford, New Jersey, after a flash flood storm, I decided to put the top down and take my wife and our two girls, about six and eight years old at the time, for a ride around town. We had a long dry spout, and the flash flood rain made the roadway slick from the residual oil. As I was stopped at a red light, the light turned green and I darted out. There was poor traction, and my wheels spun the car around. I just missed oncoming traffic by inches. Suddenly the car shot backward, and I had no steering control. The car continued to slide backward down a ravine off the side of the road. My wife and kids were screaming, and I yelled out loud in those desperate seconds, *"Jesus!"*

At that critical moment, I just imagined the car flipping over and us crushing our heads, breaking our necks, and to be all over. What did happen was the car slowed to a gentle stop, like a giant hand coming down and pulling the car to a rested position in the field just short of a maple tree that we should have hit with violent force. My wife and I looked at each other in joyous amazement. The kids were still shook up. I opened the door and stepped out to see what made the car tug to a gentle stop. Lo and behold, a strawberry patch the length and width of the car intertwined vines around the axel and wheels. A tow truck had to hoist the car out of the 8-foot ravine to a garage for minor repairs. I went back to the scene of the accident the next day to investigate and maybe pick some lucky strawberries to celebrate. Now here is the baffling discovery. I saw the deep tire marks leading up to the unscathed maple tree, and there was *no strawberry patch*!!! I looked all over the field, and there's no strawberry patch.

As far as I am concerned, some big old angel came to the rescue.

> *And to you who are troubled rest with us, when the Lord Jesus shall be revealed from heaven with His mighty angels.* (2 Thessalonians 1:7)

When I am overwhelmed with troubles, I often think back on that mighty miracle and remember the savior of my soul.

The Feather

> *Be not forgetful to entertain strangers: for thereby some have entertained angels unawares.* (Hebrews 13:2)

I pastored a church in Woodbury, New Jersey, New Life Worship Center. This was a strange group of lovable spirit-filled believers. You know the saying, "You can't judge a book by the cover." We had an evangelist, Doc Dahlquest, as part of our team. He was a motorcycle gang enforcer who by his own admission broke every commandment. He was a big mean-looking long-haired bearded man, who forsook his evil ways and gave his life over to the Lord. He was the leader of a very notorious cycle gang. Doc led a number of these thugs to the Lord, and they were a wonderful part of our worship and praise team. We gathered in the basement fellowship room, just below the sanctuary. We numbered about twelve people. We joined hands in a prayer circle praying out loud and singing hymns.

The air around us seemed electrified, and a sweet fragrance permeated the circle. Some were speaking in tongues. We were singing "Come Holy Spirit." What happened next was our voices becoming higher and sharper in pitch. We sang out in perfect unrehearsed harmony. We all lifted our heads as this radiant iridescent glow appeared above us. This incredible experience lasted about five minutes. A moment of silence filled the room, and then we lifted our clutched hands high and cheered. We dropped our hands. Just then I noticed in the center of the circle a large white eagle-sized feather! We all agreed that we witnessed an angelic presence that left us with a sign. I gave that feather to Doc who carried it with him in his evangelistic crusades.

Endless Supply

One of our parishioners, Denise, worked in the mall food court. On Sunday at the mall closing time in Deptford, New Jersey, the various food court establishments would be cleaning up their store. Any of the leftover pretzels, donuts, meat, and veggie items that normally would be put out in the trash Denise put in the trunk of her compact car. She drove to the church parking lot. At the end of our Sunday evening service, we opened the back door of the church and set a table outside with different hot and cold drinks. We supplied several cardboard boxes and bags, and people would be lining up for the distribution of the food. Remember I said it was a small compact car with a small trunk. Denise packed it pretty good, but with close to fifty people waiting to pick up food, there obviously wasn't going to be enough to go around.

PARASITIC PEOPLE

We prayed before distributing the food. At the end of praying, I again sensed the air electrified. Men, women, and children picked up boxes and walked over to the trunk of Denise's car, and we lifted food out of the trunk and placed it in the boxes.

The people kept coming, and we kept pulling food out of the trunk. Just as we thought we were reaching the bottom of the trunk and would have to turn people away, it filled up again. In the course of a half hour, people kept coming, down to the last person who walked away with two armfuls of food. There was just enough for the five or six of us volunteers to take something home.

Now after thirty minutes of constantly pulling food out of that small trunk filling the arms of I don't know how many people, the angels were helping us.

In from the Rain

It was in the mid-1980s prior to pastoring my church group. My wife and I were attending The Rock Church in Pitman, New Jersey. There was a midweek Bible study that we wanted to get involved in. When we were pulling into the church parking lot, it was pouring rain. I said to my wife, "Let me back up and drop you off close to the door, so you won't get wet. Then I will park the car and run in." She agreed and I proceeded to back up to let her off. Well normally in most cases, when you drop somebody off, your car is in drive position and foot on the brake. Here is where it is wrong and careless to assume. My car was new, and when dropping her off, she passed around the back of the car. Thinking the car was in drive position, I took my foot off the brake pedal and proceeded to put my foot on the gas to drive forward to the parking lot. Immediately the car reared up in the back. The car did not budge an inch going backward, but it alerted me to shift to drive position. The car shot forward, and I proceeded to go to the parking lot. I entered the church and sat next to my wife. She noticed me shaking and asked me what was wrong. I leaned over and whispered in her ear, "I almost ran you over." I told her what happened. Shocked by what I said, she closed her eyes and began to thank God. She opened her eyes and told me she just had a vision. She proceeded saying, "I saw angels as tall as skyscrapers forming a circle around me, looking down at me with their wings and arms by their sides."

Nothing was wrong with the transmission of my new car. At that moment, those giant angels provided my wife with all-around protection. So even in my careless stupidity, God sent his angels to protect us.

Two-Wheeled Angel

My daughter Sarina (Rini) moved to Sarasota, Florida, before me and settled in a small apartment with my grandson Ben. She took her clothes to a nearby Laundromat just off Bee Ridge Road, a six-lane highway with a center turnoff lane. There was a convenience store that she wanted to go to on the other side of this super busy highway.

She stepped off the curb and scurried across to the center turn-off lane. Before she could continue to cross the street, a luxury car was speeding and drifted into the center lane knocking Rini airborne sixty feet before smashing her body onto the concrete highway. The luxury car continued to drive away from the scene of the accident. Rini's lifeless body lay broken and smashed on the highway when this gentleman on a motorcycle stopped and got off the cycle and over to where my daughter was lying. He resuscitated her back to life. Firemen arrived just then to relieve the man who said he was a doctor. He said to the firemen that he was going to chase down that luxury car. The man took off on his motorcycle chasing down the car. Later he called ahead and alerted police that the driver of the luxury car was an 85-year-old man, high on cocaine with a prostitute by his side. The doctor said he could not hang around for the police because he had to go to another emergency at the hospital.

Rini was airlifted to Tampa General Hospital where she spent two months in critical care for concussions, broken and crushed bones, trauma, and a host of neurological problems, but she *lived*!

Her lifestyle wasn't the greatest, and it took some years in a parasitic condition to come to the realization that she needed Jesus. So all the bad that happened to her, and from her, worked out a purpose in her life. It is always darkest before dawn. She still has physical and mental repercussions from that accident. However, the spiritual benefits surpass the pain and suffering.

Oh by the way, the firemen that were at the scene told the police from their eyewitness account of the doctor on the motorcycle. The police got a name, but there was no such doctor at any of the area hospitals. I was 1400 miles away in New Jersey when this incident happened. The report by the eyewitnesses and the police report could not furnish me with a contact name or number of this doctor so I could thank him for saving my daughter's life. Was it a very knowledgeable man pretending to be a doctor, or was it an angel?

This is not the end of the story. The accident happened between 2:00 and 3:00 p.m. on Friday the 13th. Now I am not superstitious, but something happened to me on the same day and probably the same time.

Friday the 13th

As I said, I was 1400 miles away from my daughter. I was in my salon about to do some paperwork. It was around 2:15 p.m., and I was chewing a piece of prime rib. Just then the phone rang. I tried to spit the meat out onto the paper plate so I could answer the phone. Instead, the steak lodged in my throat, and it was cutting my air off. I threw myself over the back of the salon chair to maybe cough it up. I ran out of the salon down my street looking for somebody to help me. That hour of the day, most people were at work or school. I ran back to the salon. Now it was coming up to three minute with no aim, and I was starting to turn blue. I thought as a last ditch effort that I would stand in the middle of the room and fall flat on my back on the hard-tiled floor. I was thinking that the worst that could happen was I get a concussion or break my back. As severe as it sounds, the possibility of the force dislodging the chunk of meat and bringing back the breath of life would be worth it.

With just a few seconds left before choking to death, I positioned myself in the middle of the floor, spread my arms, and freefell backward. I guess instinctively my back was arched like a bow preventing my head from pounding the floor. The arch in my back must have been the key to dislodging the meat and passing down my throat, and I gasped a big breath of air—no concussion and no broken back and saved once again from the clutch of death.

This happened on the same day around the same time, 1400 miles apart from my daughter's accident both on Friday the 13th! Sounds like a good horror movie.

This incident brings two factors into play. We already know the evil on demon activity in chapter 6 and the intervention of angels earlier in this chapter. With Rini, it was a life-changing experience that ultimately turned her life around and brought her to the saving grace of Jesus Christ. As for me, the experience reminded me that while I am under the graces of God and protection of the Holy Spirit-directed angels, I was also made aware that Satan is a formidable foe. I learned never to underestimate the presence and power of darkness. As Christians, we sometimes forget that Satan (Lucifer) has been around thousands of years. He has been deceiving and telling millions of lies long before we were even born.

The power of God is far greater than the devil. However, our power is far less than that old slew foot. In *Revelation 13:7*, the spirit of God reveals to us that in the last days, Satan will overcome the saints.

> *And it was given unto him to make war with the saints, and to overcome them: and power was given him over all kindreds, and tongues, and nations.* (Revelation 13:7)

As the day approaches, evil will abound. In *Matthew 24*, Jesus answers the three questions addressed to him by the disciples: (1) When shall these things be? (2) What shall be the sign of thy coming? (3) And of the end of the world?

When you carefully read it, it pretty much describes the times we are living in.

> *And because iniquity (sin) shall abound, the love of many shall wax cold.* (Matthew 24:12)

This verse explains why we have parasitic people among us. Even though Satan and his demons are getting more aggressive now, it is because they know they have a short time left. Back to the good news! We can't fight him on our own, but we have an advocate to defeat the enemy, Jesus Christ our Champion. Yes, we overcome by the word of our testimony and by the blood of the Lamb.

That fateful Friday the 13th was an example of how the enemy attacks and how the grace of God spares us and preserves us until that time he calls us home.

There are many believers who died for the faith, and some got beheaded. God leaves one, and God takes one. In my family, there has been much heartache and loss, sickness, death, and even murder. I can tell you many more times God sent his angels to rescue me. My daughter Rini can tell you a few more. I hope to fulfill my purpose of being here. I could not do it without him. Even so come Lord Jesus.

Chapter 8

Hope for the Parasitic

Divide and Conquer

The greatest tool or tactic of the devil is to divide and conquer. If you are unmoved in your faith and the devil can't persuade you to curse God and die, his next move is to attack all that you love. He will attack your spouse, children, family, house, workplace, neighborhood, and possessions. He will attack your health, going out, coming in, talents, hobbies, and passions. He will distract what you see, hear, think, and feel. He will turn family and friends against you and fill your life with noise, sorrow, physical and mental pain, and suffering and anguish. He will make race, color, and creed like water and oil. It cannot be mixed without constantly being shaken. Satan will make people mock you, scorn you, laugh at you, and pity you to the point where all your efforts to attain peace, joy, freedom, liberty, and justice have been poured into the caldron of the futility of life.

Next time you deal with an evil parasitic person, keep in mind the characteristics and operation of the works of darkness outlined above. This is the underlying spirit that provokes the physical world we live in.

Wake up! Truth is the enemy will lose. You are the winner, and the devil is trying to bluff you. Host or parasitic person reading this, Evangelist Billy Graham with humor said, "I cheated. I read the last chapter of the Bible and I know how it ends."

Jesus warned us that if they did these things to him being the Lord and Master, how much more will they do it to you?

When the enemies of your soul seem to be prospering and gain the whole world, it is only for a moment in time, and then the judgment comes. Because I trust in Jesus here and now, I can enjoy the kingdom of heaven within me. It has been worth just having the Lord in my life. Living in a world of darkness, he brought me the light. After the smoke clears, I'll still be standing on the promises of God. I shall not be moved.

Free Liberal Spirit

In social media, the focus is on "Do your own thing"—the "I'm okay, you're okay." The host has a lot of obstacles in the way. There is no getting away from the fact that we are in a constant spiritual battle. Apostle Paul tells of this war between the flesh and the spirit in *Romans* chapter 7, verses 14 and 15:

> *For we know that the law is spiritual: but I am carnal, sold under sin. For that which I do I allow not; but what I hate, that I do.*

People in the world might argue that the spiritual world is non-existent, because you don't see or touch it. You can't see the air or wind, but you can see the effect of the wind and the air is breathable because it has oxygen in it.

Hope for the Parasitic

So we can't deny that the things we can't see or touch are non-existent. Just as we see the massive destruction of hurricanes, likewise if dark spirits are stirred up enough, widespread destruction will follow.

Opportunity Knocks

Parasitic people look for the weakest link in a chain. Here's an old saying, "Give them an inch and they take the whole arm." The *host* must be rigid and firm when setting a foundation. Jesus drew a line in the sand when the dogmatic religious leaders questioned him. There is some speculation as to what he wrote in the sand, but the spiritual significance I get from it is that Jesus was showing where you have to *draw the line*.

If you yield just a little bit to the parasitic person, you put yourself into turmoil and the parasite gains strength, because the host just fed the habit. If you really care about the parasitic person, then hold your standards high and make your objective clear. The caring compassionate person is the one most affected by this tough love approach. We don't want to upset them to the point where they become depressed or violent or contemplate suicide.

What if you leave them to their own devices? It would be a sinking ship with the host going down with them. Do you really want to save them? If so, break their cycle or pattern. Show them nice people. Get them interested in people, places, and things conducive to their health and well-being.

Chasten

To correct, restrain, subdue. Discipline is usually something that parasitic people lack. They will fight it every step of the way, because it restricts their movement. Love without restraint is a beautiful wonder to behold like a mother's love for her child. Hate without restraint is Hitler, Stalin, and ISIS.

> *Now no chastening for the present seemeth to be joyous, but grievous; nevertheless afterward yieldeth the peaceable fruit of righteousness unto them which are exercised thereby.* (Hebrews 12:11)

Using too much authority with parasitic people does not work very well. I was the prodigal son who wallowed in the mire and ate slop with the pigs so to speak. Because I was there and did that, it gave me somewhat of an edge dealing with parasites. We each have a unique role to play in ministry and in reaching out to others. My dark experiences made me keenly aware of the works of darkness. However, I have come across brothers and sisters in the Lord who worked well with drunks and druggies and homeless street people without ever having to experience that lowness. David Wilkerson, the evangelist man of God, was that kind of person who converted street gangs in New York City and himself being a simple country boy from Pennsylvania.

Reality

Not all people with characteristics of parasitic people are parasites. On every level of professional, career-minded, trade, and blue-collared works will be people who will paddle upstream against, step on, challenge, compete with, and bleed you. As that day approaches, and I mean the last days we are living in, we face danger on every side. Well I do stop and smell the roses on the way, and there are so many beautiful things to see and do. So don't mistake me for a pessimistic, negative kind of guy who goes around nit-picking and criticizing everybody. Well maybe sometimes, but I am human after all. My point is this: We are living in a constantly changing technology. Rules and values have been drastically altered against Biblical teaching. Imagine a carpenter with a tape measure that is off an inch per foot. The building will be unsafe and distorted. The same can be applied to our false standards. All this is because seducing spirits have infiltrated our society. Reversals have come about, that is, what is bad is good, what was wrong is now right, and what is abnormal and against natural order is now embraced and becomes socially acceptable. This is the new reality.

Seducing Spirits
In *Mark 13:22*, it says:

> *For false Christs and false prophets shall rise, and show signs and wonders, to seduce, if it were possible, even the elect.*

In more of today's language, we are influenced by occult and witchcraft practices on the highest level of governmental and judicial law. If you have Christian values, the powers will intimidate and mock you, control and manipulate you, and actually make you feel guilty for going against them. They will accuse the Christian of being judgmental and lacking of love and understanding. So what does many believers do? They become complacent to the point that they condemn themselves for being too closed-minded and not keeping up with modern times. *News flash!* The devil is a liar and a deceiver. He works through parasites and family and friends.

In *Matthew 24:37–39*, Jesus warns that in the time of his coming, it would be as in the days of Noah. They were eating and drinking and marrying and giving in marriage until Noah entered the ark.

Rebellion

Rebellion is the key ingredient for mayhem. There seems to be hatred for authority and order and disdain for wholesomeness and holiness. Want to pack a church? Relax your standards, give them everything they want, forget the judgmental god, and embrace the kinder, gentler, loving God that he may understand and have mercy on us.

> *For rebellion is as the sin of witchcraft, and stubbornness is as iniquity and idolatry. Because thou hast rejected the word of the Lord, he hath also rejected thee from being king.* (1 Samuel 15:23)

What Can We Do?

Now that I presented you with Murphy's law of "What can go wrong will go wrong," it was necessary to get everything on the table. If I were to actually meet Mr. Murphy, I would momentarily lose my Christian temperament and haul off and deck that sucker. More times than I like to admit, a lot did go wrong in my life with pathetically poor decisions. So now I would imagine you saying to yourself, "Well, Ron, what makes you think you can give good advice?" Here is my answer to you: I remember my mother warning me not to play with matches, because I could get burned. Well I played with them anyhow. When I did burn myself, I learned. So if you want to approach your parasite with your own method of discipline, go ahead. You may have success and more power to you. I can only suggest what I think you should do. The risk factor is small. However, Murphy's law could kick in and rob you of victory. The Bible does mention that we may not be as effective with our closest of family and friends because of familiarity.

PARASITIC PEOPLE

And they were offended in him. But Jesus said unto them, A prophet is without honour, save in his own country, and in his own house. And He did not do many works there because of their unbelief. (Matthew 13: 57, 58)

If even our Lord had trouble with the unbelief, we can expect more trouble. They questioned among themselves "Isn't this the carpenter's son?" "Isn't this the son of Joseph and Mary?"

So what are you saying, Ron??? Simply that if you are host to a parasitic loved one, it may be very difficult for you to handle them on your own. There is strength in unity. Exercise love with caution. Don't give in to their bickerings and complaining about their need to satisfy compulsive and habitual behavior. And this will only worsen chances of the parasitic making a full recovery. If you can guide them into meaningful church or social group meetings or events, it would be very advantageous.

The Choice

It comes down to the choices we make as host or parasitic. Our decisions are based on strong commitments to best shape our lives into a fruitful and meaningful relationship that complements each and joins together in harmony. Sometimes it is the host that needs to make better choices. I can't stress enough that the host is at a crossroad, where there is a fear of losing the parasitic loved one to suicide. In rare occasions, this horror may happen. One thing for sure though is that left to themselves, it may end up to a slow torturous death and much sorrow along the way, for the host, the parasitic, family, and friends that are hurt by it.

Trust

You as host need to muster up all your faith and trust in God and his ability to make right what is terribly wrong. When you try to help them, and it seems to be unfruitful, do not put yourself down. It can happen to the best of us. They have to want to change. If this doesn't seem likely, then see if you can legally force them into a program. As an alternative, do not bail them out. Be firm and do whatever it takes to keep them from self-destruct mode. I have witnessed a number of times that a substantial jail time will give them time to sort things out. *Time* heals. In a few cases, it is like the military, where it will either make or break the person. Again, it comes down to choices—*free will*!!!

The Gift

We, whether host or parasite, most often are the worst enemy to ourselves. The gift is "the present." I heard this and it stuck with me. That is why we call it the present, because it is a gift. What we do now affects our future. I mentioned this before only to stress it again, because it is a viable tool to possibly mend past mistakes or relationships. It is also a tool to correct the future outcome.

> *For by grace are ye saved through faith; and that not of yourselves: it is the gift of God. Not of works, lest any man should boast. For we are His workmanship, created in Christ Jesus unto good works, which God hath before ordained that we should walk in them.* (Ephesians 2:8–10)

It would be good to finish reading that passage of the *Scripture* from verses 11 to 22. It sums up the mind-set of God in regard to his children.

The next chapter will be several true stories of both happy and sad endings—the successes and defeats, shocks, and pleasant surprises. Names, places, and some details will be changed to protect confidentiality.

CHAPTER 9

Parasitic People
"Their Stories"

Vince and Me

Before I tell the stories of other people, which are a compilation of people I counseled with, or stories of clients and friends shared with me by permission, with changed names, places, and details to protect the rights and privacy of others, I will tell you a little about myself and a special friend growing up. My parents raised me and my two sisters in South Philadelphia. We had a summer house in southern New Jersey about twelve miles east of Philadelphia, in the town of Almonesson (named after Indians) and later to be called Deptford. The summer home was to become a home area for most of my life thereafter. I was ten years old when I met my lifetime friend, Vince Ettore. He came from Philly also, and both our fathers were professional boxers back in the old days. In fact his father, Al Ettore, went five rounds with Joe Lewis who took the heavyweight title. My dad, Joe Russo, was a middleweight champ who took the title in 1929 during the Depression. Records were not kept well during that time, so I could not get info on him. Joe Kilbane was his changed stage name. Our families struggled to survive, but we always had food on the table and a roof over our heads. Vince and I got interested in guitars and played and sang together. We had friends that joined us in singing. We had our fair share of great friends and parasitic friends.

We lost a few to drugs, to car accidents, and later in the Vietnam War. Vince was a mechanic on the copters flown into battle in Nam, while I was battling a wife and two kids starting just five months out of high school. During those few years we were separated, there was still a parallel connection though miles apart.

Before Vietnam, Vince and I were seeking God independently; and around the same time, we found ourselves witnessing to one another. We both got married and each had two daughters. The daughters were close in age and became friends growing up. We had trouble with our girls going through that parasitic stage. After years of fears and tears and prayers, our children learned through their trials and tribulations the grace and mercy of God. Vince and I saw some of our friends heading in the wrong direction with drugs and alcohol abuse. Some good friends died from cancer or the war. We both had wives who died. Even though at times we were miles apart, there was this uncanny likeness to our lives. There is so much more I could say about us, but to be brief, I would like to conclude that Vince moved to Florida, with a number of his family. I moved to Florida a half hour away from Vince with most of my family. We are quite different in our jobs and the way we use our talents and ambitions. I was more involved in the ministry with pastoring a church, prison ministry, missionary work in Jamaica, and music ministry. He on the other hand maybe wasn't as active as I was, but his faith and witness to others with the love of God was classic and admirable. Now to date we are talking about getting back into the music ministry together. Parasitic people came in and out of our lives. We still struggle with a life full of surprises. However, we always know that God works it out in all our complicated circumstances. God is not done with us yet.

Million-Dollar Baby

Her name was Marylou, and she was in her mid-forties. She was a divorcee living by herself and collecting welfare and struggling to survive. She got involved in a Christian singles group at a local church. The singles group was quite active in having international food parties with different country themes with interactive fellowship and also meeting other people and working out their difficulties, with group and one-on-one counseling with the church staff workers. It seemed like Marylou tried a little too hard to get her man and was chasing them away. Before long, she got discouraged with the Christian group and decided to advertise in a local shopping paper, looking for a date. Well a man responded to her ad and took her to a casino where she won 1.02 million dollars on the one-armed bandit. Now here is where the forces of darkness take over, and what I am about to tell you all happened within the span of two years. Her normal routine was going to church Sunday morning, but this particular Sunday at 4:00 a.m. in the morning, she won that huge bundle of money. Before she and the new man in her life can party, the Welfare representative and IRS were there to take a chunk of the win. Welfare alone took $50, 000.00 that they claimed to have paid out to her over the years. Her new man, let's call him George, claimed half the remaining money, because they had an agreement to split the winnings. In a matter of weeks, George decided that he and Marylou would not work out. They went their separate ways, and so Marylou thought that she was in a position that she could find herself another man to share her less than half wealth with. So Marylou stayed at her middle-income house and neighborhood until she could find a nicer house in a rich neighborhood. Marylou had two sons and a daughter from her previous marriage. They were all young adults. The one parasitic son heard that his mother was rich and came to visit her. He came all the way from California to New England, not to congratulate or help his mother, but only to insist that she buy him a new Harley. She did, and he immediately left to motor his way back to Cali on his new Harley. The parasitic daughter heard that her mother was rich and came all the way from Texas to visit her mom. She stayed a few months freeloading off her mom and taking drugs. She robbed her mother out of thousands of dollars and took off back to Texas. Her non-parasitic other son who lived nearby was married and working for his father-in-law. He looked in on his mom, but didn't want to impose on her for money. He was quietly struggling to pay his expenses and trying to please his wife and father-in-law. The pressure was too much on him, and he took a gun and blew his brains out.

Marylou was pretty grief-stricken over her son's suicide and became ill. She found out that she had uterine cancer, but she did not have medical insurance. She got an operation and treatment and was able to put the cancer in remission. It saved her life, but to the tune of over $100,000.00.

Marylou met Ralph whom she quickly married. Ralph suggested that Marylou invest some of her money into a business.

They bought a dough factory for one hundred grand. It was safe to assume that Marylou and Ralph would make a lot of bread (money) (pun intended). However, they did not figure out that the building was structurally unfit and it was condemned for demolition. This did not go well for their relationship. In addition to this problem, Marylou found a house in a rich neighborhood and bought it. Ralph wasn't moving from the house he had in a nice neighborhood to go live with Marylou, so they broke off and got divorced.

In the final days of this two-year period, the church committee was trying to keep in touch with Marylou to assist her in any way. She kind of separated herself from the church group and withdrew into seclusion. She was having difficulty paying the high taxes on her upper-crust house and had to go to work to try to maintain keeping up with the expenses. The church lost contact with Marylou when her phone was shut off. She never left the committee a forwarding address, and at that time the church group could not find her on the internet. She remained a mystery.

What could be said about Marylou, the "million-dollar baby"? What a tragic life after running into money. Was she better off on Welfare?

Was she looking for love in all the wrong places?

Did she make all the wrong choices without God?

Marylou was a host victim to parasitic people who used her and took her faith, hope, joy, and love away from her.

PARASITIC PEOPLE

Drinkin Lincoln

Let us call this man Lincoln. Growing up, Linc came from a poor household. His father was a heavy drinker and beat his mother when the alcohol took over. Being an only child, Linc didn't have a brother or sister to lean on and grow up with. Being raised in the ghetto of Camden, New Jersey, and white was hard for him to blend in with the black and Hispanic families and street people. Also Lincoln was the only single solitary child among the others who had multiple family members. So Linc found a way to adapt to both black and Hispanic friends. They pretty much accepted him, but not without racial slurs which were typical among young people. He became hardened and thick-skinned and would not allow discouragement or depression to overtake him. He became best friends with a mischievous black boy by the name of Darnell, who had a younger brother, Leonard, and an older sister, Tanya. Darnell was more of a prankster and practical jokester than violent and did not display criminal behavior like many of the others in the city. His brother, Leonard, however got involved with the wrong people, and Darnell and Linc together saved Leonard from dangerous life-threatening situations. His sister, Tanya, got involved with a drug dealer who pimped her off, to support her heroine addiction. Linc felt sorry for Darnell and even reconsidered the thought of not having a brother or sister. Even though there was the dark side of the family, Linc and Darnell leaned on one another and dressed each other's wounds so to speak. Lincoln didn't fair too well in high school and dropped out in his junior year. His father died that same year from liver disease from his alcohol. Linc's mother was heavy on him to bring home some money. So Linc just turning eighteen years old was playing the role of host to his mother. He managed to get a mechanic job at a local auto repair shop. His early teen years hanging around older teens fixing their cars gave him the experience. His boss, Joe, was a Hispanic man from Peru. The pay was good, but the pressure on this Irish boy from the ghetto began to wear at him. He reflected back on his life—the negative things like trying to find his identity. When he was not with his best friend Darnell, he got involved in stealing, vandalism, fights, and drugs. Lincoln not having a good role model in his life and suddenly taking care of his mother narrowly looked at women. He compared women to his mother inflicting all their needs and wants on the man. Linc previously having a fairly positive outlook on life in spite of his pathetic environment slid into a dim view of life with futility.

In the next few years, Lincoln struggled to maintain his job and get some kind of social life. His responsibilities forced changes and adjustments to his life, and he lost touch with his friend Darnell. Linc's girlfriend, Maya, was Spanish, a beautiful girl with a drug addiction. She would prostitute herself to support her habit, defying Lincoln's objections. Meanwhile Joe (his boss at the auto repair) and coworker Larry were his only audience to complain and vent himself to and to sympathize with. Together they would become drinking buddies with after-hour meetings at a pub down the street. He thought perceptively of his deceased father.

He thought to himself that the alcohol was a great escape and comfort to him as it was with his father. From there, he began to spiral downhill. He dumped Maya who at this point was strung out on heroine along with a few other short-lived relationships with other women.

Lincoln's mother met a really nice man who had a successful printing business. He (Peter) was married previously for ten years to a woman who cheated on him with his best friend who divorced her. Peter did not like where Lincoln and his mom lived and offered to have them moved into his house in the suburbs. Lincoln had just turned twenty-one and thought it would be a good fine opportunity to break away from his mom who was a burden to him and be on his own. It also gave his mother a chance to start a new life.

Linc's coworker Larry was of the same age and a single guy. So they agreed to get an apartment together. They moved to a suburb area a few miles from work and a mile from Peter and Linc's mom. Larry had a younger sister, Jenny, who just graduated high school and stopped by to check out her brother and Linc's new apartment. Now, even though Larry mentioned his sister in their auto repair shop conversations, Lincoln got to meet her for the first time. It was love at first sight. There was a slight problem though; Jenny was a church-going Christian and rooted in her faith. Shortly she discovered that Lincoln had no church upbringing and was pretty rough around the edges. Jenny invited Lincoln to attend her AG Pentecostal church. Linc hesitated at first and then asked if Larry would like to come along, so he would not feel so uncomfortable. Larry said his parents tried to get him to go to church, but he was never interested. Linc coaxed Larry to go with him just for kicks. He wanted to please Jenny. The church was full of friendly people. There was a blend of black, white, and Hispanic in the congregation. Both Linc and Larry were amused and kind of snickered at one another.

They watched the people sing joyfully and get so excited over this Jesus guy. Larry was always skeptical, while Lincoln was so overwhelmed with this new and very strange experience. Linc was bedazzled and sat there speechless, taking it all in.

At the closing of the service, Jenny's parents asked Lincoln how he felt about the church service. Lincoln felt awkward and confused. He shrugged his shoulders and said, "Well, it was interesting and different." Jenny was puzzled by his comment and asked him, "What do you mean?" Lincoln proceeded to tell them briefly that he never grew up in a church family. Jenny's parents looked over at her with that look, as if to say, "Girl, what are you getting yourself into here?" The parents shook Linc's hand. They said they were pleased to meet him and would like for him to come visit again.

Now Lincoln growing up in a far less than perfect childhood and environment was not the parasitic type and was always able to fend for himself. He did not have to depend on others. However, his mother was parasitic, and his deceased father was pretty much the same way. Lincoln at this point in time didn't know what Jenny and the other people in his life expected of him. He took Jenny to see his mom and Peter, who, in just a few short months of being together, decided that they wanted to get married.

Now Peter was Catholic, and Linc's mom came from a Methodist background. Peter was not able to remarry in the Catholic Church because he was a divorced man. Linc's mom didn't care one way or the other and saw Peter as an opportunity to have the security she always needed, and they decided to get married through the justice of the peace.

Linc took Jenny out to the movies, restaurants, and amusement parks; and they had fun together. He and Jenny soon became sexually involved, and Jenny didn't feel right about herself and her relationship with Linc. It lasted for about half a year. Jenny got Linc out to church a few more times, but to no avail. They broke up and Linc was devastated.

Linc's friendship with his roommate and coworker Larry became bitter and strained. This was due to Larry taking on a parasitic lifestyle. He was careless with the upkeep of the apartment and utilities and basically was driving Linc crazy.

Jenny went off to college in Virginia to start a nursing career. Meanwhile, Lincoln went across town to visit his mom and Peter. He was surprised to see Peter's son and daughter from his first marriage visiting there. Miriam was rather cute and a year older than Linc and sitting with her husband. Peter's son, Peter Jr., just liked to be called Junior. He was two years older than Linc and staying at his dad's house, until he could find work in the area. He was recently divorced from his high school sweetheart. They had two young daughters together, two and three years old. The daughters were living with his ex. Linc hit it off with Junior. Linc felt as though he got the older brother he always wanted. They went off to a local bar for a few drinks and bonded with one another. Junior noticed that Linc was really chugging the beers down and became heavily intoxicated. Junior offered to take Linc back to his apartment. He promised Linc that he would get his sister, Miriam, to drive Linc's car back to him in the morning. When they arrived at the apartment, Larry was there to greet them. He was high on cocaine with a hooker by his side. Junior thought it best to be briefly cordial with Larry and his friend and said his goodbyes and headed back to his dad's house. Linc's newly acquired stepsister, Miriam, drove Linc's car back to him in the morning, and Junior picked his sister Miriam up and drove back to their dad's house. Linc was hung over and really felt bad about making a lousy first impression to his stepbrother and stepsister. He went to work with Larry to the auto repair shop. Their boss, Joe, yelled at them and threatened to fire both of them if they didn't straighten out. Junior landed a nice executive real estate job rather quickly and got his own apartment on the other side of town. Junior invited Linc over to his place several times and took him out to a bowling alley. He also took him fishing together. Junior tried to avoid the nightclub scene with Linc. He was even concerned when Linc drank one too many beers on the fishing trips. Junior was just a social drinker and once in a while would smoke a cigarette with Linc.

Larry would tag along with them at times, and it began to wear at Junior's defenses. The toxic personalities of both Linc and Larry and bad habits even wore down Junior's productivity at the real estate office. He knew at that time that he would have to nix his relationship with Linc.

Linc's mom meanwhile was becoming troublesome to Peter. She started drinking a lot at home and got overweight and lazy. Lincoln was not getting along with Larry who was forsaking sobriety for more and more drugs. Lincoln who at one time played host to his mother and Larry had now become a burden to himself. He was becoming a victim to parasites, in turn rendering Lincoln a portion with the parasites and much turmoil. Junior thought about helping Lincoln and maybe even offering sharing his apartment to get Lincoln away from Larry. He excused the idea from his mind because he thought about his dad having a difficult time with Linc's mom. He saw it as a crisis increasing with intensity. His younger sister, Miriam, now pregnant and just a few months away from giving birth, asked Junior from time to time about Lincoln. She had her responsibility to her husband, but out of compassion she wanted to help Lincoln in some way. So Miriam decided to make a large pot roast with all the vegetables and brought it over to Lincoln. Linc choked up inside as he took it from her. He never experienced such compassion and thoughtfulness before. He asked Miriam if she would like to stay and join Larry and him at the dinner table.

"No, thank you," Miriam replied. "I really must get back to prepare dinner for my husband." Linc thought to himself, *Why can't I have a woman like that?*

A few years went by and Miriam gave birth to a baby boy, now three years old. Junior got engaged to a woman that he sold a house to on the other side of town. She kept the house in a divorce settlement, along with her sweet little five-year-old daughter in her custody. Junior moved in with her. Linc's roommate, Larry, was fired from the auto repair shop and took another job working at a department store stock room. Linc was drinking heavier and distanced himself from Larry who was now into heroin big time. Lincoln an alcoholic and Larry a heroin addict strained their living conditions and relationship. Then it happened. Linc came home one night to find Larry dead on the floor just next to the door. The law stepped in and interrogated Linc for his alleged involvement with Larry, and they trumped up enough charges to land Linc in jail for several months.

In jail Linc was better off, because he could finally be kept from his liquor and Larry. He enrolled in a rehab program, and after several months, he was released. The auto service station job was still there, but his boss Joe hired a new guy in his absence. There wasn't much for Linc to do, and he felt awkward staying there. Then a break and opportunity came his way. Darnell, his black street buddy he grew up with, bumped into Linc at a convenience store; and they both got engrossed in conversation inside and outside the store. Darnell told him that he landed a nice job driving a truck for a moving company. Darnell pulled some strings for Linc to get a commercial license and work with him in the moving business.

Linc lost his old apartment and belongings. His stepbrother, Junior, got him a nice apartment near him; and Linc seemed to adjust to his new job and place.

"The Awakening of Drinkin Lincoln"

Lincoln got his commercial driver's license with help from his old friend Darnell, and they worked together in the moving business. They got to talking a lot, and Linc just had to know how Darnell managed to stay clean with a bad brother and sister and living in poor conditions with a poverty-stricken family in the ghetto. Darnell, after hearing Linc's many questions, finally spoke.

"Let me answer you with a few questions I want to ask you."

"Okay shoot," Linc replied.

"Did you ever hear me curse, or take drugs, or steal, or go around busting heads?"

Linc replied, "Why, now that you said it, I don't remember you doing any of that?"

Darnell proceeded to tell Linc that it was because of his grandmother who was a shouting Pentecostal woman of faith. He said she instilled Christian values in him and it sustained him and gave him strength to face seemingly impossible odds growing up. Darnell said his grandma handed him a Bible and asked him to promise her that he would read it. She passed away shortly after that; and Darnell, though very heartbroken over her death, noticed the peace and hope she possessed. That was when he invited Jesus into his life.

I can write a book on Lincoln's life story, but I will conclude his story saying that the moment Darnell told his story was when Linc was broken and became a new lump of clay molded in the Master's hand. He remembered his girlfriend Jenny tried to share her faith with him. He looked her up. He found she finished her nursing degree and was working in a nearby hospital. They got together again and married a few months later, had three kids, and lived a happy life together. Together they changed the lives of most of the people mentioned here.

To God be the Glory, *Amen.*

Chapter 10

Addressing the Host

Heartbroken for America

Before I can address the people who have played host to a parasitic society, I must first address the condition of our US of A as it is viewed and treated by the rest of the world. The land I love that our early fathers shaped by the moral code and standard found in the Bible. It framed the Constitution that kept our country in the graces and blessings of God.

We as people and government have departed from our original determination to be one nation under God with liberty and justice for all. Our freedom and rights are questionable to say the least. Our dreams and ambitions have been thwarted by political and religious dogma. In our quest for pleasing everyone, we forsook what is right. In trying to please everybody, we failed in pleasing ourselves. We thought that we have to deny ourselves and not be selfish. The truth of the matter is that we neglected our self-preservation. Our intentions were pure, but our standards were compromised.

There is no rule or measurement to go by; just do your own thing and "I'm okay and you're okay" philosophy, when in actuality we are not okay with ourselves nor are we with others. The world hates because we thought we could buy them by buying their goods and win their respect and admiration.

PARASITIC PEOPLE

We thought we could police the world and proclaim that we will make everything alright. However, in essence, we are drowning in our own deception and complacency. The internal strife with discrimination, hate, racism, and political anarchy is far worse a threat than the outside world. We don't want to fight for any causes. We just want to sit back hoping the world will sort out their own problems and leave us alone to relax and eat popcorn and watch TV and play on our computers. The enemy is building up outside our haven and fortress, and we are unaware of our pending demise.

Oh how I pray that our political, religious, and racial differences would somehow find a path of understanding toward love and compassion and peace. Who are we fooling? Human nature has a penchant for greed, lust, power, and superiority.

America is at the crossroad. We can change or go down in flames like Sodom and Gomorah and Babylon and Rome did. It was always said, "If we fail to learn from history, we are doomed to repeat it." Remember what our soldiers fought and died for. Don't let their ultimate sacrifice be in vain.

Was September 11, 2001, the handwriting on the wall for America like it was for ancient Babylon? Ancient Babylon was a nation of people surviving several hundred years. Israel was a captive people under the rule of Babylon and was a city of sixty square miles. It had a 300-foot high wall extending fifteen miles wide by fifteen miles long. The Euphrates River passed under one wall and exited under the far wall fifteen miles away. It was a wall the Babylonians thought could not be penetrated. The Babylonians became complacent people who wanted to trade goods and buy goods from their enemies to avert war and make the enemy content enough to leave them alone. The whole reason they built the wall was because the many years of trading and buying wore thin and the enemy nations surrounding them wanted the treasures of great Babylon. The Babylonians thought that the unrest they experienced with the outside world would be a threat to their economy and safety. They thought that cutting trade with the rest of the world would create jobs in their country and boost the economy. They had everything within their walls and didn't need to rely on the rest of the world for anything.

Now on the surface this logic seems to make sense. We think to ourselves, *The rest of the world hates us and is jealous of us and wants to destroy us.* The Babylonians thought that they were safe within their own borders and they didn't have to fight anyone or even be concerned with the world outside their walls. Why? We can draw from our own natural resources and use our well-educated and wise people of our land and grow and prosper and be mighty.

The one thing that the Babylonian logic overlooked was that they were unaware of the hostility brewing outside their walls. While they were in pursuit of their worldly desires and luxuries, the enemy outside the walls were fortifying their military and studied their holidays and celebrations.

The day of reckoning came when Babylon forsook principles of conduct toward God and their fellow citizens. On one of their greatest holiday celebrations, the guards and magistrate got drunk with liquor. Darius the king of the Medes and Persians diverted the river Euphrates to go around the wall and not under the wall. Neither the guards nor anybody else in the city noticed the river go down. The vast army of men passed under the wall and gate and took the city in one night (portions taken from *The Cambridge Ancient History* archives).

Compromise

It is so subtle how the enemy will draw a person into a comfortable false sense of security. In many instances, compromising certain situations seems to be the solution to creating a mutual respect and consideration, especially with neighbors. You would not want your dog barking and yelping loudly in the middle of the night, waking up your neighborhood and vice versa. Nor would you want kids trashing your property. There are guidelines to consider and proper conduct to consider and a proper attitude that creates an atmosphere of harmony in the home and workplace. However, here is where the line has to be drawn. Jesus demonstrated this by drawing a line in the sand and writing on it. Of course much is speculated as to what he wrote, but what is to be made clear is where you have to make a stand on principle and proper ethics to prevent possible destruction of all you aspired to accomplish. In the Old Testament Bible stories Lot compromised with his wife staying in sinful Sodom until his wife and that city were destroyed. Samson compromised with Delilah and met his doom. Aaron compromised with the sinful people making idols of gold until Moses rebuked him.

Now that we have an example of the downside of compromise, let us move forward to more specifics of what not to compromise: *not* when it supports parasitic habits and addictions, *not* when it supports parasitic behavior and abuse, and *not* when it could possibly lay waste and/or destroy all your hard work and dreams and hopes.

Draw the Line

Tell others and convince them and yourself with great conviction that yes is yes and no is absolutely *no*. It is the law of *no* when assertively applied that will define the boundaries that are enforced and observed. When that boundary is compromised, the host opens Pandora's box so to speak, to wreak havoc, sorrow, and pain on any future plans.

In the next chapter, we will go into depth about the power of *no*.

Chapter 11

The Power of No

It has often been said in church circles that God answers prayer in three ways:

1. *Yes*, I was waiting for you to ask me.
2. *Yes*, but be patient and wait awhile.
3. *No, I love you too much!*

It is the "*No*, I love you too much" that we naturally reject at first, but later we find out that what we asked for would have been bad for our body, soul, and spirit. Like children, we pout to God because we assumed he did not have a problem with our prayer request. What we did not know is that we do not see the unforeseeable events that would have taken place in our lives which would have resulted in a very negative experience.

An example of this "*No*, I love you too much" is when I tried five times to move to North Carolina. I did ask that people pray for the Lord's will and not necessarily my desires. That was a good thing because the places I picked were flooded out or in a bad area or near a trash site.

When it involves a close loved one like a parent to their child, at whatever age, *no* hurts. It hurts both. Truth of the matter is, if you said *yes*, it might be something you regret for a long time. I remember the TV commercial that was I think an auto repair ad. "You can pay now or you can *pay* later." Emphasis on paying later means paying a lot more money. I will use my stupidity as an example. I made the mistake of co-signing for someone close to me that left me with nearly $8000.00 to satisfy the payoff amount. I knew the Bible warned about such dealing, yet I did it.

Now before I relate a few stories to you, I don't want to get carried away with labeling every person that thinks or does things wrong that they are automatically called parasites. I certainly don't think that I am perfectly without fault when it comes down to making decisions that are disastrous. We all make mistakes but come to a point in our lives where we see we went wrong and seek to make it good. "The school of hard knocks" mentioned before became our closest friend. My sister Margie related a story to me about our parents.

Margie had a bad marriage with her first husband and had three children with him. Without getting into personal details, in short, my sister came running back to our parents when things constantly went wrong with her life. My parents did everything they could to protect, feed, and provide solace and shelter for her. Well after years of enabling my sister through this, that, and the other, my mother got to the point where she could not take it anymore. At that juncture in my mother's life, she realized that her daughter's problems were affecting her life with my father and the life they vowed in marriage and commitment to one another. Then the one-liner that mom addressed to my sister was the turning point in my sister's life.

"You Made Your Bed, Now Lie in It"

My sister had to pack and leave quickly. She proceeded to tell me that she struggled at first and went on Welfare for a while. After a little while, she took on a waitress job that she had to beg her boss for. I guess the desperate tears broke the man down, and she became a great waitress and made out very well on tips. It was at that time my sister Margie realized that she unlocked the potential that was hidden in dependency on others. She advanced to modeling and secretary jobs and gained her independence.

My sister's two daughters turned out very well, and my sister said it was because she was too poor to help them, so they made it on their own.

I got to thinking about what my sister Margie said about being too poor to help her daughters, hence making them more independent early on. Now my sister Anna and I did just the opposite, and we showered our children with the last dime in our pocket if need be to get our children established. And they took our last dime over and over again.

My sister Anna and I suffered many tears and frustration over our children. We both realized how futile it was to throw good money after bad. We found out late in life that we enabled, aided, and abetted our children to continue pounding us until we broke down. It was at that time something clicked in my head and I said *no*. My sister felt the same way and now has no problem saying *no*.

So you see I waited till the eleventh chapter to reveal to you that I played a major host to parasites surrounding my life. The saying "Do what I say, not as I do" does not apply to me. It is "Do what I say, not as I did." I feel like such a fool; but if going through what I went through ministers to one who reads this book, it would have been worth it all. I would not change a thing because the experience brought me to the place where I am now. As I move forward in this life, I am seeing the fruit of my labor. Things are changing before my eyes that I never thought possible. The experiences work out for the better when we put our trust in God. It was when I leaned on my own understanding that I got myself into trouble. It is the flesh wearing with the spirit. So often we put ourselves in harm's way and all because we imagined how things would turn out and it is never what we expected. Even the time factor seems to drag on longer than we had hoped for. When the results finally come, we are pleasantly surprised.

Respect

Respect is to feel or to show honor or esteem for or to show consideration for, honor, or esteem (Webster's Dictionary).

Hmmmmm. So if the parasites don't respect you, in essence they are not honoring what you say or do, nor do they esteem you in your opinion, nor your values, nor your standards and beliefs. In other words to put it bluntly, and somewhat crudely, "You're screwed!"

Once this attitude with the other party is established, it would be very difficult to turn that disrespect around, but not impossible. Now we have to get down to the real nitty-gritty and hold our ground when the conflicts arise. And believe me they will arise. Be prepared with the understanding that it may cost you something. In some way it may cost you time, money, pain and suffering, humiliation, inconvenience, and embarrassment.

The times we live in are a very different world now than back in the 1950s. WWII was over and the war babies came into the mix, creating families with at least three or three children. Ahhh, the family unit was strong and they sat at meal together and discussed school and preparations for college or a trade. And if the child did not show respect to the teacher, they would have a bigger problem when they got home.

Matthew 10:34–36 speaks about Christ not coming to send peace, but a sword. It sounds contradictory at first but goes on to explain in verse 35 that he will bring variance between family members. In other words, bring the family members at terms and conflicts with one another. In verse 36, it says that a man's foes shall be they of his own household (KJV). So there you have it—an expression of the times we live in.

It is a part of human nature to live in denial of things that go wrong in our lives. It is common to respond negatively when somebody asks you, "How are you doing today?" The response would be "Great" or "Pretty good" or "Okay, I guess." Now that last one really means "Not okay," but they don't want to get into it, unless you inquire and show some interest. Unfortunately, the average person lies six times a day unknowingly. If you tell people you are doing okay and you really are not doing okay, you are lying. Now realistically when we ask people how they are, we are not expecting a negative response. So here is where it gets tacky. Are we prepared to face this negative response? Now we can do one of two things: (A)

Ignore the negative response or change the subject hoping not to get involved or (B) sit down or take a moment to lend an ear and talk to, listen to, and comfort the person. Either you lend a shoulder to cry on or offer advice or some possible solutions.

Independence

Remember the greatest way to make the parasitic person self-sufficient is to assist but not enable them to depend on your constant assisting. Say, for instance, you have a son or daughter that will soon be getting out of spending a few years in prison. Now there is a few things you can do:

(A) Take them in to live with you, with the intention that they will only stay a couple of months to get established and leave. (B) Maybe another friend or relative of yours would be willing to take them for a little while and then be off on their own. (C) Or take out a loan if you have to and help them with the security deposit and two months' rent.

Take a moment and think what would be the wise choice.

Okay, let us pick apart the choices.

(A) Taking them in to live with you for a while. Hmm, well you are gambling with the idea that they would stay until they get to the point of taking care of themselves and don't need any more help. The problem with this would be that they learned to develop a system of living blending your rules with some of their own. Well, you might ask, "What is wrong with that?" Plenty!!! You made a comfortable nest for these birds to take the worm from your mouth and waiting for you to fly away and bring back more worms to feed them. Because they are still dependent on you to supply their need, they expect an easy life where someone else will be there for them. Before you know it, they will have one excuse after another and count on you to continue to assist them. If you think you can set a date where they will have to leave, "good luck." You may find yourself in there for the long haul.

(B) A friend or relative would take them in for a while. Well the same applies to them, like it did with you in the above set of circumstances. What makes this much worse is that you may drive a wedge between you and your friend or relative. This could turn out to be quite tragic, and I know for a fact that the situation turned out fatal for a family I knew.

(C) Take out a loan if necessary and pay their security deposit and two months' rent—the wise choice. If you weigh in the balances and the initial cost to you while providing an opportunity for your loved one to sink or swim, on their own independence and recognition, it would weigh in your favor as well as theirs.

So in conclusion to "independence," make sure you play out the scenario in your mind before you make a decision. Your life, your loved ones, and your relationship with those close to you will make an impact.

Respect

This thing or whatever you want to call it is the most important part of our life. If you don't respect yourself, how are you going to expect it from others? We have talked about self-esteem earlier in the book and how parasitic people lack this image and disregard it toward others. However, even though you have this respect for yourself, it can backfire on you, due to lame decisions you made, allowing the parasitic person to test or challenge. Respect is a high standard that is an expected behavior, attitude, and consideration that forms the boundaries. If you relax your standards, then you are in for the long haul of abuse and neglect. Because you relaxed your standard, others will take advantage of the opportunity. The host opens Pandora's box of tricks and challenges that would drive you insane, if allowed to go on for long periods of time.

Compromise

This can very easily be the very tool of the devil to bring down your fortress. In other words, you relaxed your standards. This is not to be confused with mutual consented guidelines. It is an agreement to respect each other and not cross over the line. When *Jesus* drew a line in the sand before the religious Jewish leaders and his disciples, there is speculation as to what he wrote. Now instead of formulating or inserting a thought or commentary on what he wrote, I would rather fix my attention to the line he drew.

The line represents the boundary that was put in place to show that crossing that line is crossing the boundary. When the boundary is crossed, then it activates a negative response that is counterproductive and transgresses trust and unity. Here is where compromise relaxes high standards and opens the door to hostile behavior. Compromise sounds like a nice word, but underneath it all, you gave way to uncharted territory.

Dark Territory

So now we see that crossing the line and relaxing standards and compromising bring us into dark territory. So what do I mean? I mean that you know your thoughts and rules and standards and where you draw the line, but you can speculate all you want about the person you are dealing with. However, you don't know for sure their thoughts and views on life.

The Dark Heart

What does dark heart mean? We can start with the phrase "a career criminal." Some people aside from being the parasitic type have a criminal personality. This kind finds the easy way around or out of a situation. Convenience, as opposed to legal, "bends the rules" to solve the problem. A strong 85 percent to 90 percent of those that come out of prison after four or five years are most likely to end up back in prison. Years ago was a lot easier to adjust to present-day lifestyle and circumstances. Now technology is moving so fast that it is even hard for me to get used to a new cell phone. Privacy is a thing of the past; and if you are on the internet a lot, and especially things like Facebook, you are exposing yourself to much scrutiny. When these people are released into the new and strange world, they gravitate to old acquaintances. These old friends and relations are their connection to the new world. The only problem is that these familiar people had a profound influence in their lifestyle that landed them in jail in the first place. I know that as a host to these people, it is hard for you to accept what I am about to say, but please listen carefully. If you

PARASITIC PEOPLE

don't see these people forming new relationships and approaching life from a different perspective, then the experience you will have will be very disheartening.

Unless their whole outlook on life is a turnaround, with a new beat and music, you will be caught in the same old syndrome of heartaches and disappointments as before their original prison sentence. Often it ends up worse than before. I am not saying that you should be cold-hearted against a dark heart, but I am saying that if you let your guard down, you can get slammed against the wall.

Lend an ear and advice from a moderate distance. Muster up as much wisdom to keep yourself from entanglement, but at the same time assist with a strong assessment to keep yourself from drowning.

The dark heart is not a community parasite and is a loner. They think they have control, but lose control when reality strikes. Be cautious.

The *dark heart* makes an effort to reach out with good intention. The problem here is trying to adapt to their new circumstances, but make the fatal mistake of staying friends with old acquaintances that are parasitic in nature. They need to change the parasitic environment as I mentioned earlier as becoming a breeding ground.

> *And, behold, I come quickly, and my reward is with me, to give every man according as his work shall be.* (Revelation 22:12)

A Host Conclusion

Learn how to say *no* to things that you know will hurt you and them. I outlined the pros and cons and gave you possible outcomes, but the reward awaits those that do the right thing.

Remember

Excuses are the culprit that stops the healing process. The word "addiction" is a negative word that means you are hooked which seems like there's no way out. If you treat it as a 0 bad habit, it changes the playing field so to speak. The truth is that in order for the healing process to begin, it starts with a new mind-set. How come, if alcoholism is a disease, it is the only disease that comes in a bottle and you can get ticketed for or wind up in jail over? You see it is quite simply a behavioral problem and has to be addressed as a head problem and outlook on life that must first change. You have to say *no* to excuses and *yes to seeking God* and trust to find within yourself the goodness that comes from a positive, whether *host* or *parasite*. All that I wrote in this book won't amount to a hill of beans if both parties don't make a sincere effort to work out the problems with mutual respect. I tried to show you the side of you and me that there is a time, frail and vulnerable and frightening with uncertainty and fear. Also, I tried to show how faith can overcome the negative assaults. Through the toughest of times and seeing down the road, even the most horrible of circumstances turns out to be a big blessing. Read Bible verses about *trusting* God and finding peace in his word.

> *Trust in the Lord with all your heart and lean not on your own understanding; in all your ways submit to Him, and He will make your paths straight.* (Proverbs 3:5, 6)

Wisdom before smart, compassion before bitterness, and love before hate.

About the Author

Ron Russo was born again in 1971 and ordained through Full Gospel Assemblies, Coatesville, Pennsylvania, in 1991. He is currently involved with a partner Mario Vitali in promoting amateur and professional Christian entertainment (individuals and groups) and a musical play production *Rock & Scroll Trilogen*. He is a former inter-denominational Pentecostal pastor, evangelist, and missionary in Jamaica. He was involved in prison ministry and Christian counseling and a singer/musician recording artist and pioneer of Christian rock. He sheds light on the biblical perspective of dealing with and ministering to people who need hope and a new life.

CPSIA information can be obtained
at www.ICGtesting.com
Printed in the USA
BVHW070429020119
536776BV00013B/1583/P